Emotional
Prosperity

—

Jason Vallotton

EMOTIONAL PROSPERITY
A Practical Guide to Counseling

Scripture quotations marked (ESV) are from The ESV® Bible (The Holy Bible, English Standard Version®), copyright © 2001 by Crossway, a publishing ministry of Good News Publishers. Used by permission. All rights reserved.

Scripture quotations marked (NIV) are taken from THE HOLY BIBLE, NEW INTERNATIONAL VERSION®, NIV® Copyright © 1973, 1978, 1984, 2011 by Biblica, Inc.™ Used by permission. All rights reserved worldwide.

Scripture quotations marked (NKJV) are taken from the New King James Version®. Copyright © 1982 by Thomas Nelson. Used by permission. All rights reserved.

Emotional Prosperity: A Practical Guide to Counseling is written solely as a pastoral guide to counseling and is not intended to take the place of professional education and training in the field of psychology or counseling.

Cover Design: Amy Miller
Internal Layout: Jonathan McGraw

support@emotionalprosperity.org

Table of Contents

Foreword

BY DANNY SILK

Since the late 1980's I have been a professional helper. Before that, I was just good at it. I can remember sitting around a dining room table with my mom, aunt and grandmother, all of whom were single at the time. As I sat there listening to them all talk about the "man" problems they shared, I could hardly not say what seemed obvious to me at the time. The advice I gave made them all turn to me and stare. My grandmother was the one who said, "Danny, I think you should be a counselor someday." I had never heard that word before. I was nine.

The "helping" profession isn't for everyone and yet everyone will end up facing a situation where someone they know needs help. It reminds me of when Jesus says, "Many are called but few are chosen." Many will be called upon to give advice, support, counsel or encouragement, but not all will actually enjoy it. Some people are just born to help. These people know they've been put on this earth to see others get through to the other side of their pain and challenge. They feel chosen for "such a time as this" each and every time it finds them.

Even the "chosen" are looking for tools. Tools that bring it all together. Tools that help them to help others learn to help themselves. Tools that make complex life issues turn into bite-sized problems people can actually solve. Tools that overcome powerlessness, fear, and doubt. Tools that give hope.

Emotional Prosperity: A Practical Guide to Counseling is this kind of tool. Jason Vallotton is one of these real helpers in the world who knows how to show people the way to the other side. He has a gift to bring people through their pain and to courageously face the fear they experience. Having lived through it, he has shown so many others how to seek healthy emotions and find freedom.

One of the beautiful elements of this material is that Jason knows who to help. He knows that not everyone who is experiencing pain or creating destructive consequences around them actually wants help. Even people who shout, "SOMEONE HELP ME!" don't always want to be helped. Jason also knows why people need to face difficult realities. He understands that there is a process each person must face about their lives. Jason is able to discern when a person is ready for an answer, and what will be helpful for them to do in order to move forward. The author of this book will show you how to get help and how to help the people in front of you who have a problem and want a solution.

Watching someone find freedom is one of the greatest experiences I've ever been a part of in my life. I've seen some tremendous physical healing miracles. I've seen a near-blind child get perfect sight back. I've seen a woman born deaf hear her mother's voice for the first time.

I've watched a 15-year-old boy whose ribcage, set on his hip bone from scoliosis, straighten up right in front of me. But I still have to say that the healing power of forgiveness and the rescue from anxiety and depression are still among my most favorite things to witness. And then be a part of equipping someone to keep those demonic experiences from ever returning feels like one of the greatest victories on this earth.

I am happy to recommend the following pages to you and am confident that you will receive what you need to lead others into emotional prosperity.

——

Danny Silk

President of the Loving on Purpose Life Academy
Author of *Keep Your Love On, Culture of Honor* & *Loving Our Kids on Purpose*

SECTION ONE

Identify

Lesson One
PREPARE FOR A SESSION

My love for counseling came to me at a very young age, before I even knew what "counseling" was. I grew up in a community where leaving the ninety-nine to chase after the one was the norm, sometimes literally! In a small town, the only thing that travels fast is gossip. There was no need to confess your sins one to another, because usually by the time you mustered up the courage to tell all, everyone already knew. My parents oversaw homegroups and church activities for more than 20 years, so as a family, we were always deeply entrenched in the dealings of church life in a small town. Looking back, I can clearly see how the Lord had positioned me as a young man for the role I serve in today.

In the 6th grade, I had an experience that significantly shaped who I am. One evening after dinner, I sat at our large oak table listening to my dad tell stories about King David and his mighty men.[1] Storytelling was one of the most anticipated activities for our family, mostly because of my dad's endless and hilarious childhood feats, and his ability to make you feel as if you were actually there. As the evening turned to night, I found myself hanging on each word my father spoke, leaning in as the plot thickened. David had gained access to King Saul because of his reckless abandonment to God. All on his own, David had snatched a helpless lamb from a starving lion, conquered a bear by the strength of his hands, and overpowered an entire army with a sling. David was not only a man's man; he was the people's hero!

Enraged by jealousy, King Saul went mad and tried to kill David, pursuing him like a wild animal through deserts and caves. While David was on the run, outcasts from other cities began to flock to him by the hundreds as a source of protection. As time went on, these so-called "outcasts" began to be transformed into mighty men because of David's influence on them and his devotion to God. It is said of these mighty men that one was as a thousand

---

1 See 2 Samuel 23.

and two was as ten thousand. Because the hand of the Lord was on David, God eventually delivered him from Saul's wrath. He went on to become King over Israel.

This story about David is incredible; however, that was not what changed my life. That night as I listened to my dad, I had a revelation that I was like David (minus Saul). I was a young man anointed by God, and I had been put on this earth to help transform the "outcast" back into who God had originally created them to be-- mighty! My heart burned like coal as the reality sunk in: *This is my purpose in life, the reason I was born!* It was then that my love for the "one" was birthed.

Fast forward two decades, thousands of counseling appointments, and several heartbreaking events in my life. I have found that my love for people has only increased through the years, thus giving me a desire to take what I have learned and impart it to you. I pray that as you work through this manual, what took me years to learn would become easy for you, and that together, we could transform the lost, hurting, and broken people of this world back into their God-given identities. My challenge to you is to find Christ in each person that you minister to and to do as Paul instructed us—reconciling them back to the Lord just as Jesus did for us, and not counting their trespasses against them.[2]

Considering Clients

As you begin this workbook, it is important to know that the tools provided herein will help you to be successful in various types of counseling situations. However, while everyone can benefit from counseling, there may be times when a particular client is not a good fit for you. In order for both the counselor and the client to have a positive experience, conducting a proper intake assessment before an appointment is scheduled is wise.

---

2 See 2 Corinthians 5:18-19.

REFLECT

Scenario: You get a phone call from Ava, a member of your church, requesting a meeting because she is having difficulties in several areas of her life. She attends church on a regular basis, but you do not know her very well. The extent of your interactions with her prior to this request is the smile and handshake she gives when leaving the sanctuary on Sunday mornings.

What would you typically consider before setting up a meeting with Ava?

_____

_____

_____

_____

_____

_____

_____

_____

While there is no *right* methodology behind preparing for a session with a client, there are several considerations that can be very helpful. If you are the sole counselor in your environment, you may even need guidelines that will help you choose which clients to counsel, as there may be more need than you have time for! The following are some great questions to ask yourself so you can determine what you might be getting into.

———

Is This a Request or a Referral?

It is important to note who is requesting the meeting. A person will either request a meeting for him or herself or come as a referral from a third party. The tone of the meeting and your approach will differ accordingly.

1. **Requests** for appointments are made by people who have recognized a need for help in a specific area of life. A person requesting a meeting may ask for an appointment because they are facing a difficult situation or are noticing a destructive pattern in their life. This proactivity in seeking help indicates a willingness to receive counsel and a measure of ownership.

2. **Referrals** come from a third party who is suggesting that someone get help. This dynamic can be interesting because the potential client may or may not actually *want* help. For example, if a family member or overseer refers someone to you, it is wise to ask the person making the referral to encourage the potential client to contact you directly. This ensures that your first connection with your client comes by their own initiative, a small but significant step towards taking ownership of their situation.

   Here are some good questions to ask the person making a referral:

   - Why do you believe this person needs pastoral counseling?

   - What behaviors are being displayed?

   - How long has it been going on?

   - How have you handled these behaviors with the client?

   - Did it work?

   - How many times have you confronted him/her?

   - Is this person open to real and honest feedback?

   Here are some good questions to ask the person being referred once they contact you to make an appointment:

   - Why were you referred to me for counseling?

   - What is the nature of your relationship with the person who referred you to me?

   - Do you believe counseling can help you move forward?

Who is the potential client?

It's also a good idea to gather some basic biographical information during your intake process. Information can include but is not limited to:

- Family history and birth order

- Health history (basic mental, physical, emotional health)

- Relationship status

- Major traumas

- Work

Learn as much as you can about your client before the meeting so you can make the most of your limited time with them. Knowing who the client is will help you build a framework to understand their area of need.

What is the Problem?

It's important to know the nature of the problem before the first appointment. If a client can give a brief description of the area in which he or she needs help, it will help you prepare for the appointment. Here are some helpful questions and space to write your own:

- Why are you requesting counseling?

- How long have you had this problem?

- What have you already done to work on this problem?

- Who in your community has been walking through this process with you?

- _____

- _____

REFLECT

Scenario: The Young Adults pastor at your church forwards you an email from Juan, a college student in your congregation. While Juan does not display any destructive behaviors, several sentences in the email suggest that Juan is not in a good place. The Young Adults pastor thinks he needs counseling and hopes you will know what to do.

Given your consideration of the scenario, how would you direct the young adult pastor to proceed?

_____

_____

_____

_____

_____

_____

_____

In a referral-type scenario, it's important to "seek to understand" before offering advice. It is wise to ask the person making the referral whether or not they have actually addressed the perceived problem with the potential client. In the scenario described above, I would suggest that the Young Adults pastor connect with Juan in person because connection facilitates the building of trust and safety. When the pastor addresses his concerns about Juan's emotional state, he should use language that sounds something like this: "Juan, thanks so much for the email last week. Would it be okay if I asked a few questions in regards to what you wrote?" From a place of connection, it would be appropriate for the pastor to suggest some counseling, and Juan could choose whether or not to seek help.

As you gather information during your intake process about the nature of the request, the potential client, and the situation at hand, it's important to be honest with yourself about whether or not this client is a good fit for you. Perhaps they need counsel in an area in which you're not qualified to help. Or perhaps you find out that you'd do well to study up on a certain topic before the appointment based on the issue at hand. A good intake process is an essential part of considering clients and preparing for a counseling session.

Preparing Yourself

Personally preparing for a counseling session will be different for each counselor because every person has different needs. The quality of your preparation will determine the quality of your counseling. You will need to *know* what you need in order to be successful, *check* to make sure you're at your best before meeting with a client, and *value* the gift God has given you to approach the task with confidence.

Know Yourself

In personally preparing for a session, it's important to know what you need in order to be at your best. For example, if you find it helpful to have time to clear your head before meeting with someone, then you will need to plan to show up early. Take the time to set up your office to suit your needs, and eat a good breakfast if you find that you are mentally foggy without having had a good meal. These might seem like no-brainers, but the more intentional you are about bringing the BEST you to the appointment, the better.

REFLECT

Considering your personal needs, what are three things you know you need to do in order to be well prepared for a counseling session?

1. _____

2. _____

3. _____

Check Yourself

Before you begin an appointment, take inventory of how you are doing internally. I have found that my worst appointments are those that I go into with anxiety or stress. Often I think I'm dreading the appointment, but when I take a moment to acknowledge and address my emotions, I find that other factors are usually at play. If you've had a stressful day, you're having struggles with friends or family, or you just didn't get enough sleep the previous night, acknowledge the facts and give attention to any issue that may negatively impact your ability to counsel your client.

You could start by asking yourself a few questions:

• How do I feel?

• What can I do about it?

• What do I need in order to approach this appointment with peace?

Ultimately, you want to make sure you are free and clear from any emotional or environmental distractions before you invite a client into your office.

Value Yourself

Being aware of who you are, your identity as a son/daughter of God, and the reality that people's expectations of you do not determine your worth is crucial to good counseling practices. No one is going to give you value; your value comes from God. Because He values you, you can value you. Having value for yourself gives you the ability to value others. Confidently approach the task at hand knowing that He is the giver of the gift inside of you, and He says that you're worthy of love on your best day AND your worst day!

> *You cannot go into an appointment with your identity in question.*
> *The only way I can walk into a meeting not feeling anxiety is to*
> *have my identity in tact. I am rooted in the truth.*

Invite Wisdom

As you prepare for a counseling appointment, remember that you are not entering it alone. You have the greatest Helper on your side; you have Wisdom in the room! Your job is to listen, both to your client AND to the voice of Wisdom in order to navigate your appointment with discernment.

PRAY

Wisdom, I invite you into this counseling session to be my Helper. Holy Spirit, you are the greatest Counselor, and You know how to help this person more than I ever could. Be with me, lead me, direct me, and guide me through this session. Show me how to help this client. Amen.

Create a Safe Place

Once you have personally prepared for a session with a client, you will want to focus on creating a safe place for your client. There are a few different elements that go into creating a safe place, including preparing the room where you're hosting the appointment and setting the tone for the meeting.

Prepare the Room

Making sure the room is ready for your client can go a long way to ensure they feel comfortable and safe. The physical atmosphere is just as important as the spiritual atmosphere in a counseling session. When a room is aesthetically pleasing, comfortable, and non-threatening, it invites the client to enter and be at peace.

There are many things you can do to prepare the room including the items listed below. Feel free to add your own ideas to this list.

- Make sure the temperature is comfortable. A good room temperature for most people is 71-73 degrees Fahrenheit

- Provide a cushioned seating area

- Be seated where eye contact is easy for you and the client

- Remove any distracting objects from the space

- If possible, provide a bottle or glass of water for the client

- Have tissue within arm's length of the client

- _____

- _____

- _____

Set the Tone

As you begin the appointment, you can enhance the atmosphere of safety by expressing to your client that you are excited about the appointment. This verbal affirmation lowers tension, reduces assumption, and sets clients at ease. It is also a great idea to pray as you start the appointment, reminding yourself and your client that God is bigger than any challenge they are facing.

People want to be loved, comforted, and nurtured. As a counselor, you can facilitate this. Keep in mind that unless you already know your client, people won't necessarily know your personality, and it could be difficult for them to determine if you are straightforward, quiet, or sarcastic. You don't want your client to be distracted by having to pick up clues and indicators to figure out how to read you, so it is a good idea to let them know a little bit about you, your style of communication, and what they can expect from the process.

Not only will your client be getting to know you, YOU will be getting to know your client! It's important that you are willing to take a look at their life without judgment or assumption because assuming you already have someone figured out will disable you from truly listening.

Display these three very important attributes in order to set a healthy tone in your meeting:

- **Empathy:** The capacity to understand or feel what another being is experiencing from within the other being's frame of reference; the ability to put yourself in another's shoes.

- **Sympathy:** A feeling of care and understanding for someone in need.

- **Compassion:** A deep sense of care for someone in need, which motivates us to help.

You have probably heard the saying, "People don't care how much you know until they know how much you care." If you can enter into a person's experience, people will actually feel loved and cared for. Once that is established, you can begin the process of helping.

Empathy, sympathy, and compassion are so powerful because they give you the opportunity to link arms in the journey of life. When you partner with God's unconditional love for a person, He will show you how He sees them, and there will rarely be an offense you can't look past.

REFLECT: A COUNSELING STORY

In 2007 I worked as a pastor in a ministry school. My job involved caring for sixty-five students ranging from 18 to 80 years of age for nine months of intense ministry training. The first day of school was filled with the buzz of excitement as new students filtered into our environment, ready for adventure!

As each one arrived, I greeted them with a hug and a few questions about their life. This was usually a great way to break the ice and create a platform for connection, but it didn't go as well as I'd expected with one student in particular.

REFLECT: A COUNSELING STORY *(continued)*

LeAnn came all the way from London to attend our school. She was a beautiful woman in her early twenties and seemed to have it all together. I eagerly approached her as I had approached thousands before her, but when I leaned in to give her a hug, she instantly pulled away and said, " I'm sorry, I don't hug men!" Right away I could feel the tension between us. I hadn't done anything wrong, and neither had she, but her reaction was way outside of my cultural norm. Not wanting to make it any more awkward for either of us, I quickly backed up and said, "No problem, I'm sorry!" The conversation ended as quickly as it started.

In my heart, I felt that something wasn't quite right with her, but I had no concrete evidence, nor did I want to assume anything just because she had laid down a boundary inside of our relationship. That day I made it a goal of mine to build trust with her over the next nine months.

Over time, LeAnn watched how I treated the other women in our group and how careful I was to respect her needs. After several months, she finally opened up to me about her past and the violations that had taken place, causing her to not trust men. I took my time carefully walking LeAnn toward freedom as she gave me permission. Had I rushed in to help her after our first interaction without building trust, she might have never opened up to me. I spent days listening to Wisdom, creating a safe place, seeking to understand, and modeling real love, all before addressing any of her issues.

Today, LeAnn is not only free herself, but she's helped hundreds of other women and men into wholeness just like her. There cannot be enough said about starting an appointment correctly, because how you start something almost always determines how it will end.

Describe how you would connect to each of the following words in regards to LeAnn's story based on what you've learned about creating a safe place for your counseling appointments.

Empathy: _____

_____

_____

_____

REFLECT: A COUNSELING STORY *(continued)*

Sympathy: _____

_____

_____

_____

Compassion: _____

_____

_____

_____

Communicate Clear Expectations

If you don't take time to set expectations for the meeting, they will be set for you! Every client will come to their appointment with a range of expectations. For example, the more entitled someone feels to a meeting, the higher the expectation they will set. If someone has had negative experiences with counseling in the past, they may have very low expectations that keep them guarded or wary. Regardless, expectations that go unmet can lead to misunderstanding, which is counter-productive to your goal of helping people!

While you want to be clear, make sure you create space for clients to interact with you about the process. Give them permission to have a voice if they don't understand something. We will discuss how to set clear boundaries in later sections of this manual, but here are some initial steps you can take to lay out the ground rules for your appointments:

• Ask clients to be on time.

• Ask clients to come prepared with something to take notes. (If they show up unprepared, ask them how they plan to recall the information discussed in the appointment.)

- Explain to your clients that if you give homework at the end of an appointment, you will only set another appointment if their homework has been completed so as not to waste time. Mutual investment is necessary for success in the counseling process!

- If you have not committed to ongoing counseling appointments with this client, explain how many times you plan to meet with them and what the process will be.

REFLECT

List three ways you can intentionally create a safe place for clients.

1. _____

2. _____

3. _____

Emotional Chemistry

You can have the greatest education and credentials, but if you are unaware of the emotional chemistry that needs to take place between you and the person you are counseling, the session will *not* be a success. As much as the counselor analyzes the emotional health of the client, the client equally "analyzes" the therapist. Often times we see the role of a therapist portrayed in movies as passive, disengaged, or reserved. In an actual session, if the client experiences a therapist as cold and detached, they will not feel the bond and trust necessary to expose their deepest feelings and fears.

Tone and Mood Matching

You do not have to have known the client for years previous to the session to feel this connection; in fact, that wouldn't be helpful. It is your responsibility to match the client in tone, mood, posture and enthusiasm. If you have a client who is cracking jokes, meet them right back there. If they are quiet and reserved, match their tone and create a safe place. If they are sitting arms wide open and relaxed, then position yourself to be open as well. If they are in a ball on the couch, don't invade their personal space. Sit back and give them space. It is in their ability to feel connected to you that your clients will experience breakthrough. No one wants to open up to a wall. If you are stone cold and blank-faced, you will be no more enticing than a stranger on the street.

Non-verbal communication is one of the loudest and most predominant forms of communication. This communication tells others you are going to understand them or that they are wasting their time being there. Ultimately, nonverbal communication is the greatest factor in your emotional chemistry, which will in part determine whether your client wants to be in the session with you or not. Keep in mind that you don't have to be fake in order to match a client's mood--the goal is to make them feel known and comfortable and to provide a safe place to be heard. People can force themselves to do something they don't want to do; however, this won't last long. If you want your client to commit and see health, they have to feel like they connect to you.

Counselor Vulnerability

If you notice your client is not opening up, take a break from trying to "go somewhere." Stop for a moment and observe the mood. From there, share something real about your life that could pertain to the conversation. Sometimes people just need to know they are not alone. Your personal story of hope, understanding, and being a real human may be the key to getting them to go deeper into freedom. It is okay to share real and vulnerable things as long as you have already worked through them and won't need your client to turn into a therapist as you share your story.

REFLECT

Scenario: Suzie is in a session with you. The session is going moderately well, but not as well as you hoped. She is sharing but doesn't seem to be opening up her heart to the painful areas that need to be explored. She is in the middle of a story about her last relationship and the painful abuse she experienced. One moment she is sharing, but the next she stops and says, "It doesn't matter, it's over now."

It is in that moment that you decide what happens next. You can move on to a new subject, or you can stop for a moment to comfort them and let them know they are not alone in this process. It's important to know that sharing from your personal story has the potential to create a codependent relationship by making yourself the source of their hope or comfort. From time to time you can give just enough detail from your own story to help them know they are not alone, but not so much that you become their source for getting their hope and needs met.

Making sure your client understands that they are not alone in their process or pain is so important. People tend to think they are the only ones who have ever experienced their situation, so if they can realize they are not, they can experience an overwhelming sense of hope and vision.

It is in these moments your client can bond with you. There are many boundaries to consider between the client and counselor, such as relational professionalism, not crossing any sexual boundaries, and avoiding a co-dependent long-term relationship, but if there is no sense of knowing and being known, the client will not want to return.

In addition, the client must feel like they are respected and seen as a whole person by their counselor. They already know they are there for counseling, so they don't need to feel like the one person in the world that is supposed to help them sees them as a lost and broken cause already. You are there to treat them with respect and believe in them where they have lost belief in themselves. You are the voice inside their head telling them they can make a change and not fail. If you see them as broken, they will never see themselves as becoming whole.

Remember, stepping into their point of view and perspective will allow your clients to feel safe. No matter the behavioral issues, mental disadvantage, and emotional numbness they may be experiencing, you are their advocate. You are not the judge.

Advocate Versus Judge

Being someone's advocate is the greatest tool one can have as a counselor. In the counseling world, you will often find that some of the greatest counselors discern very well. They can sense the issue, point it out, bulldoze over the process, and jump straight into the issue the person has and what they need to do to change it. To the counselor, everything is so clear, as if the issues are seen as easy as 1,2,3. However, with that mindset, judgment can be a predominant undertone. The person on the other end of the session will be hearing, "This is so simple, why didn't you see this before?" or even worse, "You're such a screw-up, even this stranger can see all your faults." If you are counseling someone who has had a rough past and done some extremely destructive things, you need to be aware of your tone, posture, facial expression, and mood.

A simple way to keep all of these non-verbal communication factors in check is to go into your session with an advocate mindset. If you are someone's judge it will be impossible to have compassion, because judgment kills compassion. However, if you are there to be an advocate, you will be able to step into their process with them. You may be the first person who hasn't seen them with disgust as their story is told. You will become the safe place they want to return to. You will build trust with clients when and only if you are there to be their advocate.

This is such a crucial piece of counseling, so be aware of your inner dialogue. It will be difficult to advocate for them if you are thinking things like, "If you had only done this, you wouldn't be here" or, "You're so weak, blind and broken. Poor person. You have so far to go." Those are very judgmental thoughts, no matter how valid they may seem. You are there to encourage, uplift, lead, and envision your client through the pain and the long process into health and freedom. This will only come from compassion and belief on your part.

 **REFLECT**

Take a moment to write down a few of the factors you have experienced in your own life that left you feeling connected and inspired or disconnected and discouraged. We have all had conversations, whether with a counselor or a friend, that made us want to draw closer and continue the conversation or that made us want to run and hide. Focus on the non-verbal communication and emotional chemistry you experienced.

_____

_____

_____

_____

_____

Make a mental note to pay attention on a daily basis to those around you that seem to connect and have emotional chemistry with others, and those that don't. You want to become a master at connecting and creating emotional chemistry as the success of your client will depend on it.

Closing Keys

Preparing for a counseling appointment begins long before your client sits across from you and shares their story. In order to effectively begin a counseling appointment, remember the following keys:

1. Consider clients with care.

2. Prepare yourself by knowing, checking, and valuing who you are while inviting Wisdom to guide you.

3. Create a safe place by preparing the room, setting the tone, and defining expectations.

4. Remember that as the counselor, you are there to be the advocate for your client, not the judge.

NOTES

Lesson Two
IDENTIFY THE PROBLEM

First Things First

In counseling, it is important to remember this simple but profound truth: **You cannot help someone who doesn't think they have a problem.** The process of identifying the nature of a problem starts with the client's recognition that a problem actually exists. However, that a person has made an appointment with you is not necessarily an acknowledgment of a problem in and of itself.

Once you begin the appointment, you must start the conversation to get to a place where you AND the client can identify the problem at hand in order to solve it. Be sure to move at a pace that is comfortable for your client. As you begin communicating and asking questions, remember that the goal of the conversation is understanding.

Communication is Key

Good communication is an art, and most of us aren't born knowing how to communicate well. We want to learn to become excellent communicators, especially in our line of work, so that we can equip our clients to communicate skillfully as well.

Becoming a good communicator will ensure that you know how to:

- Help people feel powerful, validated, and heard

- Lower anxiety

- Create a safe place for a connection or solution to be established and maintained

Like most things in life, the more you practice, the more skilled you will become. As you work through this lesson, we will cover basic teaching on communication styles and tools that will help you sharpen your own communication skills, keeping in mind that these principles will apply as you work with your clients too.

Four Styles of Communication

1. **Passive:**

   Passive communication implies, "Your needs matter and mine don't."

   People who operate in this style often avoid expressing their feelings, believe they are not worth taking care of, allow themselves to get run over, and lack confidence due to fear.

2. **Aggressive**:

   Aggressive communication implies, "My needs matter and yours don't."

   People who operate in this style often violate and dominate other people in conversation. This style is fear-based, like passive communication, but the fear manifests in aggression.

3. **Passive-Aggressive:**

   Passive-aggressive communication implies, "I will say that your needs matter, but I will act to protect my own."

   People who operate in this style often feel weak or resentful and often sabotage, frustrate, manipulate, and disrupt. This style is also fear-based in that the communicator tries to appear compliant, but for fear of not being taken care of, acts to protect himself.

4. **Assertive:**

   Assertive communication implies, "Your needs matter and so do mine."

People who operate in this style express their needs and wants clearly and respectfully. They understand that they are in control of themselves and can have good boundaries. This style of communication is rooted in love and is based on the understanding that we are all valuable in our needs, ideas, and desires. Assertive communication is the healthiest style.

REFLECT

Scenario: Tom tells his wife, Barbara, that they should go on a date this weekend and asks her what sounds fun to her.

Read Barbara's possible responses, and label them as passive, aggressive, passive-aggressive or assertive.

1. "Fine. I'm choosing the restaurant because you always pick gross places." _2_

2. "I would love to go out to dinner, but do you have anything specific in mind?" _4_

3. "Whatever you want to do is fine with me. You choose." _1_

4. "It doesn't really matter to me, I just hope that it's fun." _3_

"I" Messages

Assertive communication maintains that both parties are powerful and both parties have valid needs and feelings. In conflict situations, it's important to communicate clearly and concisely to let the other party in on how you're feeling in order to create space for resolution and re-connection. One of the best ways to do this is through the use of "I" messages. It's easy to accuse and make assumptions when feelings are hurt, but limiting yourself to "I" messages will help you tell the other person about yourself rather than make assumptions about them. Often times, when a peaceful conversation escalates quickly and both people are feeling judged and defensive, it is because the parties involved do not know how to use "I" messages. When working with your client, be sure to take time to explain what an "I" message is and how to properly execute it.

- **"I feel..." messages:**

  DO SAY: I feel misunderstood and sad after that conversation we had the other day about making the bed.
  DON'T SAY: I feel like you didn't understand me the other day when we had the conversation about making the bed.

- **"I think..." messages:**

  DO SAY: I think I need to understand how you feel.
  DON'T SAY: I think you're angry because you don't want to make the bed.

Chart Your Maps

I-maps, You-maps and We-maps are simple tools that can enable you to become aware of how you and others operate best inside of relationship. These mentally noted or written observations can help you navigate relationships more successfully by being aware of what each person needs. Used properly, these maps will allow you to nurture your fondness and admiration for one another by allowing each of you to "show up" and be known in the conversation. Be sure to take time with your client to write out their own personal maps as well as any others that might be relevant to the situation.

- **I-map:** Get to know yourself well!

  - How do you process information?

  - How do you like to communicate in order to feel connected to the person with which you communicate?

  - What do you need in order to feel safe in communicating on a vulnerable level?

    Ex. I am a very practical and concrete thinker, so when people ask me how I'm doing, I default to talking about what's on my calendar rather than my feelings.

- **You-map:** Intentionally learn about a person in order to understand and love them the way they receive love best.

  - How do they process information?

  - How do they like to communicate in order to feel connected?

- What do they need in order to feel safe and fulfilled in communicating on a vulnerable level?

  Ex. My best friend is a very abstract thinker, so when I ask her how she's doing, she defaults to talking about her heart, dreams, and feelings.

- **We-map:** Enables me to understand the nature of my important relationships. I intentionally gather information about you and me, which allows me to understand *us* better.

  - What are our major differences?

  - What do we need in order to communicate effectively?

  - What common connection points do we share?

    Ex. In order for my best friend and I to feel connected when we talk on the phone, we need to talk about practical things as well as our hearts and feelings.

Words for the Wise

The following tools will help to create successful communication in relationships. Take time to practice these so that you will be able to effectively communicate with and teach these skills to your client.

- **Soft Start-Up**

  - How you begin will usually determine how you end.

  - Starting softly with kindness and gentleness keeps hard conversations palatable because the other party is disarmed.

- **Look for Win-Win Resolutions**

  - While there may be no perfect solution, a win-win resolution accounts for and considers both parties' needs and brings balance so each party gets *some* of what they want or need.

  - Work to avoid win-lose resolutions, but in certain instances where one party truly doesn't care about the outcome, win-lose may be appropriate and acceptable.

- **Repair Attempt**

  - A repair attempt can be any statement or gesture that attempts to calm, diffuse, or end a conflict peacefully. Repair attempts can be used in any relationship to prevent negativity from escalating out of control. This could include an attempt at humor or a gentle ask to start over with the acknowledgment that neither party is enjoying the moment.

  - Married couples will benefit greatly from using this tool. Repair attempts are the secret weapon of emotionally intelligent couples.

  - You can read more about "repair attempts" in the book 7 Principles For Making Marriage Work by John Gottman.

- **Seek to First Understand, Then to be Understood**

  - Seeking to understand is crucial to ALL good communication. Keeping this principle in mind can change the outcome of a conversation.

REFLECT

Scenario: Paul and Linda have been seeing you for a few weeks regarding their inability to communicate well with each other. They come to you for advice on how to navigate a certain conflict. Paul is upset with Linda because she did not pay their electricity bill on time, and there seems to be a pattern of dropping balls that are hers to carry. Paul responded compassionately, and together they made a plan for how to get everything done by working together.

What is an example of a <u>soft start-up</u> that Paul could use to initiate this conversation?

_____

_____

If the goal is to use <u>"I" Messages</u> rather than telling Linda what she has done wrong, what could Paul say?

_____

_____

When Linda replies to Paul's "I" Message to express his frustration, Paul learns that Linda has been feeling really overwhelmed by the number of to-dos on her plate. What would be a possible <u>win-win resolution</u> for this couple?

_____

_____

The Art of Listening

The foundation in all good communication for a counselor is the art of listening. In a conversation there is always a speaker and a listener; the majority of the time, the counselor is going to be the listener. The process of listening involves more than just hearing someone talk. Listening involves following the thoughts and feelings of another person and empathizing with his or her perspective. Listening requires that you pay attention to the message communicated beyond the words.

―――

Reflective Listening

Reflective listening is a practice by which you do not offer your perspective, but rather carefully remain focused on the speaker's message. This is an important skill to possess as a counselor because truly focusing on the client's message and having the ability to reflect back to them what you've heard is a way to ensure that both parties understand what is truly being said.

Here are the two steps in reflective listening:

1. Listen to what the client is communicating with their words, facial expressions, and body language to the best of your ability.

2. With words, reflect back to the client the thoughts and feelings you heard in his words, tone of voice, body language, and gestures.

Ex: "Wow, Micah. Let me make sure I understand what you are saying. You are feeling powerless because your emotions are taking over at inopportune times. Am I hearing you correctly?"

To be a good reflective listener, you have to keep yourself out of problem-solving mode and simply listen for the message being delivered, how it's being spoken, and what's *not* being said. Reflecting back to the client what you've heard them say can actually help your client clarify their own thoughts, feelings, and emotions! It can help them learn how to articulate more accurately and clearly while moving into deeper levels of learning how to express him or herself. Reflective listening will also help you clarify your goals and purpose as you move forward in your sessions together.

REFLECT

Think about a time when you shared your heart with someone when it felt as if they were disengaged. Explain how that made you feel and what they could have done differently in order to make you feel heard.

_____

_____

What is the primary difference between listening and reflective listening? Why is one more effective in a counseling situation than the other?

_____

_____

Become a Great Question-Asker

Once you grasp the basics of effective communication and how to become a reflective listener, it's important to hone your question-asking skills! I can think of a few people in my life that are naturally excellent question askers, but typically this is a skill that gets better with practice and intentionality. You can choose your questions based on the direction you want to go in your counseling appointment. Different types of questions will lead you to varying degrees of understanding the whole scope of the problem. There are a few keys to remember when asking questions:

- **Get the Facts Straight:** If you're trying to understand basic factual information, ask questions that are narrow in focus and specific to the client or situation. As you receive answers, follow your curiosity to ask questions that might further your understanding of the scope of the problem.

  ◦ "If you could get one thing out of this appointment, what would it be?"

  ◦ "You referred to something horrible happening when you were six years old. What happened to you when you were six?"

- **The Heart of the Matter:** If you're trying to help someone connect to their heart and emotions, ask questions that require them to open up. Acknowledge their vulnerability, and ask deeper questions only after you've established some connection with the client to make sure they feel safe. Open-ended questions will prompt your client to search themselves for answers and lead them to a more comprehensive conclusion.

  ◦ "Emotionally, how are you doing?"

  ◦ "How did that make you feel?"

- **Multiple Choice:** Some people may have a hard time with abstract, open-ended questions, especially if they're not used to connecting to their heart and emotions. You can give them multiple choice questions if they're having trouble finding words.

  ◦ "Does it feel like pain, anger, or frustration?"

  ◦ "When you lashed out in anger, do you think it was because you were afraid of being misunderstood or afraid of being rejected?"

- **Never Assume:** Ask questions. Never assume that you know what your client is thinking or feeling. It's important that your client feels powerful and understood during your appointment.

  ◦ "Does this statement feel true to you? 'I won't ever amount to anything.'"

  ◦ "It sounds like you might be feeling hurt. Is that right?"

Good questions are empowering and unassuming. If a person can answer a question for himself, then he will own his answer forever and take steps to do something about it.

REFLECT: A COUNSELING STORY

A couple of years ago, I had a group of BSSM students who decided to drink alcohol while on the campus of a local Christian university. One by one I invited them into my office in order to see if they were willing to take ownership for their mistakes, clean up their mess, and protect our environment. As the first person sat down on my couch, I decided to take a really soft approach because I could see that she was incredibly nervous and clearly "on guard." After offering her something to drink, the conversation went like this:

Me (J): How can I help you?

Student (S): *I don't know!*

J: Well, why are you in my office?

S: *I guess I'm in trouble...*

J: Oh! You are?

S: *I guess so, I got caught drinking last night at Simpson University.*

J: What's the problem?

S: *I got caught drinking at Simpson.*

J: So the problem is that you got caught drinking at Simpson?

S: *Uh, well I guess, right?*

J: I don't know. Did you know that drinking at Simpson was wrong?

S: *Well, kind of.*

J: Kind of? So you're not sure if you knew that drinking at Simpson was wrong?

S: *Well, I knew it was wrong, but I guess I didn't really think about it.*

J: So you knew that drinking at Simpson was wrong?

S: *Yes.*

J: Why are you okay with violating your conscience?

S: *Um, I don't know. I didn't know I was violating my conscience.*

J: What did you get out of violating your conscience?

S: *Um, I'm not sure.*

J: Well, why did you decide to drink last night?

S: *A couple of us went to a bar to play pool, so we had a few drinks, and afterward we went to Simpson. While we were at Simpson, our friends pulled into the parking lot next to us and offered us some beer. We were really far away from the main campus, and I didn't think it was a big deal.*

J: But you knew that drinking at Simpson was wrong, right?

S: *Yes.*

J: So last night when you were hanging out with your friends, what did you feel when everyone else was sharing a beer?

S: *I guess I felt like I wanted to be a part of the group; I wanted to be included.*

J: Ahhhh, so you were willing to violate your conscience in order to feel accepted?

S: *Yes, I guess so.*

Going into this meeting, I was really aware that I could threaten them with being kicked out of school or shame them for their behavior, which might have forced her and her friends to stop drinking. However, I knew that simply stopping the drinking was not going to solve the deeper issue. By coming in with a soft startup and asking good questions that helped me understand where she was at, I was able to help her see the larger problem. Once she identified and owned the fact that she violates her conscience in order to get acceptance, we were able to give attention to the wounded areas of her heart that the Lord wanted to heal in order for her to experience freedom.

Use Yourself As the Plumb Line

Good questions are the doorway into a person's inner world, but merely extracting information from an individual doesn't necessarily help them move forward. One of the most challenging aspects in counseling is knowing what to do with the information you are given. It is easy to get caught up in writing down every sticky detail of a person's life but actually miss the key answers you're looking for. When I listen to someone share their story, I pay close attention to what strikes me as "odd" or "off" using my own life as a plumb line.

Basically, if anything seems weird, incongruent, inconsistent with Scripture, or unhealthy, I write myself a note about it so that later I can ask more questions to see if their answer leads me to a root issue. Over the years I have learned that if it seems "off," it probably needs attention.

REFLECT

Scenario: Anthony comes to counseling because he's struggling with masturbation and can't seem to identify the reason behind the problem. Here are the steps I took in asking questions, using myself as a plumb line.

Question: *What is the problem?*
Answer: *I struggle with masturbation.*
Question: *What were you feeling before you last masturbated?*
Answer: *I was feeling lonely.*
Question: *Can you tell me more about that?*

NOTE: Compare this to what you know of your own life. For example, "When I feel lonely, I don't masturbate. Lonely for Anthony and lonely for me are probably two different things." You are the plumb line; whatever doesn't feel quite right should pique your interest.

Given the scenario above, what would be your next question?

_____

_____

Trust yourself in the counseling process. You are more capable
than you know of helping someone find a way to freedom.
Pave the road with good questions.

Closing Keys

Once someone has identified that they have a problem and ask for help, you initiate the journey of getting to the bottom of it! Great communication tools are necessary to navigate the conversation with your client. Communication involves both speaking *and* listening well! Sharpening your communication, listening, and question-asking tools will benefit you greatly in learning to become a great counselor.

NOTES

_____
_____
_____
_____
_____
_____
_____
_____
_____
_____
_____
_____
_____
_____
_____
_____
_____
_____
_____
_____

Lesson Three

BELIEF SYSTEMS AND CYCLES

Belief Systems

A belief system is a set of interrelated and mutually supportive ideologies that we maintain in order to develop and define our personal sense of reality. Simply put, belief systems can be depicted by the stories we tell ourselves about how the world works and who we are inside of it. It's possible for two people to have identical circumstances but entirely different experiences, due in part to the belief systems through which they interpret their circumstances.

For example, every person experiences a sporting event or movie in their own way.

When watching a basketball game, what one person sees as a "great play," another person sees as a "foul." Their viewpoints on the play are usually determined by their belief system about the teams.

There are many things that contribute to the construction of a belief system over a person's lifetime, including a person's collection of life events, family history, cultural norms, and peer pressures. For this reason, belief systems, even if unhealthy, can be very difficult to change.

Identify the Current Belief System

To identify and understand a client's current belief system can be key in knowing where to start in breaking free of unhealthy patterns or bondages. In light of the reason your client is in your office, there a few things you can to do identify a client's current belief system in order to determine if they are living in any unhealthy cycles or thought patterns.

- **What's their history?**

  Understanding a person's past is crucial in understanding the context for their present.

  - What's their family background?

  - What's their cultural background?

  - Is there a history of past trauma?

  - What's their relationship like with their parents?

  - What's their relationship like with God?

  - How do they relate to authority?

  - How long have they been dealing with their issue?

  - What have they already done to work on their issue?

- **What are they saying?**

  - What is your client saying about themselves and their situation when they are speaking freely and unfiltered? Their language and tone can help you understand what they believe to be true.

    Ex. "I always mess up relationships. I'm so stupid."

    (Words like always, never, and every are great indicators of deeply ingrained beliefs. Also, self-judgment is typically part of a belief system as well.)

- Are they saying what they really think, or are they saying what they think you want to hear? Sometimes what people say and what they actually believe are two different things. Especially in religious circles, it's not uncommon for someone to say the "right" thing and disregard their true feelings. It's important to listen for inconsistencies.

  Ex. "I haven't been able to sleep because I have so much anxiety about my finances, but I really trust God."

  (It's impossible to REALLY trust God for a situation and have anxiety over it at the same time.)

- **What are they thinking?**
  - It's possible to identify what a client consciously believes according to his or her level of certainty about a topic.

    Ex. If your client struggles with pornography and says something like, "all men struggle with pornography," you can see that a belief system is empowering his negative behavior and undermining his freedom.

  - Subconscious beliefs are often more indicative of our belief systems than our conscious beliefs. Asking quick-fire questions helps clients respond out of their subconscious belief system instead of their logic. The human brain will automatically want to give the "right" response to every question instead of giving a heartfelt, genuine answer, so true beliefs are often revealed by making someone respond without having time to think it through. When using this tool it is best if your client is comfortable and knows what to expect. Be sure to explain what you are doing and ask for permission before you start. Let them know this tool is not going to be spiritual nor is there a wrong or right thing to say. You simply want them to relax and answer the questions as quickly as possible. Here's what it can look like:

Quick-Fire Questions:

Counselor:	*Close your eyes. As I ask you some questions, I want you to fire off the first thing that comes to your mind.*
Client:	*Okay.*
Counselor:	*Are you ready?*
Client:	*Yes, I am.*
Counselor:	*What do you believe to be true about tigers?*
Client:	*They are awesome!*
Counselor:	*What do you believe to be true about pink elephants?*
Client:	*They are not real!*
Counselor:	*What do you believe to be true about fun?*
Client:	*Hard to find.*
Counselor:	*I am going to keep going, so close your eyes again. What do you believe would happen if we find a problem?*

Client:	*I'll fix it.*
Counselor:	*What do you believe to be true about intimacy?*
Client:	*It's painful.*
Counselor:	*What do you believe to be true about friends?*
Client:	*They'll leave.*

Powerful people are not victims of a God-ordained plan for their lives.
If someone says, "I trust God with my life" but lives in chaos, then
something is out of alignment. You cannot have anxiety and God
in the same room because He is the Prince of Peace.

REFLECT

According to the example above, what conclusions can you draw about this client's belief systems in the following three areas of his life?

Fun: _____

Intimacy: _____

Friends: _____

In the above example of how to use quick-fire questions, I want to draw your attention to the client's belief about fun. He said that fun is "hard to find." When you get a response like this, take note of it! You would stop here before moving on to other quick-fire questions to address the problem. You can use a number of different counseling tools that we will discuss in later lessons in order to find the root cause of this negative belief system. Ultimately, finding the root cause will empower the client to repent and make changes to move forward in freedom.

The goal is not to ask a million questions; the goal is to ask the
right questions and know what to do with the answers.

Identify Trigger Points

Once you know what a person believes in their subconscious about a certain topic, you can begin to identify trigger points. This is an important part of the process of changing belief systems. A trigger point can be any person, circumstance or thought that catches you off guard in the moment and causes an involuntary reaction. Trigger points, when pushed, instigate the reaction a person has to unmet needs, familiar trauma, and potential pain.

Here are some common trigger points for people:

- feeling unaccepted
- feeling disrespected
- feeling out of control
- feeling worthless

- experiencing injustice
- feeling controlled
- feeling lack of love
- experiencing challenges

- feeling disoriented
- feeling ignored
- feeling a lack of resources
- feeling familiar pain

People respond in a variety of ways when you talk about pain. There are people who will laugh while others will deflect the questions. Each person can display different indicators of pain. For example, some people believe that trauma is hard to get rid of, and someone who has experienced abuse might say, "It doesn't matter how I feel; it's never going to change." A different person who experienced the same trauma might display carefree, flippant attitude and say something like, "I'm fine! I live in a different universe now. That experience happened a lifetime ago." Identifying a client's belief system often happens when you see how they respond when they are triggered.

REFLECT: A COUNSELING STORY

I worked with a man named Ray who told me that he called himself an idiot on a daily basis. This piqued my interest because this man was far from an idiot. First, I decided to figure out how he came to believe that he is an idiot and why he currently believed it. When I heard his story, a few key things popped out, and I was able to engage him in a line of questioning. Here are a few of the questions I asked him

REFLECT: A COUNSELING STORY *(continued)*

- How long have you thought this about yourself?

- When did you learn you were an idiot?

- What triggers you to say this to yourself?

- What have you done to try to change it?

The answers to these questions were really insightful. Ray told me that when he makes mistakes, he calls himself an idiot. The declaration, "I am an idiot," is a manifestation of self-judgment triggered by perceived failure. I was convinced he was a very kind, intelligent, generous man, contrary to his negative self-talk. He was just in the habit of judging himself outside the bounds of God's love. Recognizing the trigger helped identify his belief system, which led us to attack the problem at the root.

What are a few quick-fire questions you could ask Ray in order to find out what he believes to be true about failure and how it's affecting his self-talk?

_____

_____

_____

_____

_____

HEALING TRIGGER POINTS

Ultimately, every person would like to be free from trigger points. While the process might be long, it is possible for trigger points to change the same way an overall belief system can. To work on eliminating triggers from a client's life, start small.

- **Make a list of triggers**

  A person might not know all of their trigger points right away, but they will know the ones they react to the most. These are the ones that catalyze the most emotions or cause a person to shut down.

- **Choose the top 3**

  Have them choose the top 3 things from the list affecting their lives the most negatively. Instruct them to reflect on these questions when those trigger points are pushed:

  - Is this reaction logical?

  - Do I have a specific need that would be beneficial to communicate in this situation?

  - Could it be that I am taking this too personally? If so, should I let it go?

  - What do I need to do in order to feel powerful in this situation?

  - What is God's perspective about how I'm feeling?

  *All personal breakthrough begins with a change in beliefs. The moment
  we begin to honestly question our poor belief systems and the experiences
  we assign to them, we open the door to replacing our old, disempowered
  beliefs with new ones that will move us forward.*

REFLECT

Scenario: Samuel feels angry every time his boss walks by him in the hallway without acknowledging him. He has developed a belief that says, "My boss hates me."

Using what you just learned about trigger points, how could you help Samuel?

_____

_____

_____

_____

_____

Scenario: Mary sweats profusely, breathes heavily, and feels disoriented every time she has to speak in front of a crowd, causing her to feel embarrassed.

Using what you just learned about trigger points, how could you help Mary?

_____

_____

_____

_____

_____

EMOTIONAL PROSPERITY

CYCLES

Belief systems are like ecosystems where thoughts are formed and behavioral cycles are established. Some cycles are healthy while others are the direct result of unhealthy belief systems that perpetuate destruction. It's important to ask yourself, "Is my client living in any unhealthy cycles, or is this problem they are facing an isolated situation?" More often than not, you will find that the client has some sort of perpetual cycle that can be identified.

Healthy Cycles are cycles formed in positive environments where healthy self-image encourages positive attitudes, high expectations, and good behavior, which result in successful performance and reinforced positive self-image.

Unhealthy Cycles are formed in negative environments, which foster negative self-image. A negative self-image leads to negative attitudes. When we have a negative self-image and attitude, we naturally have lower expectations for ourselves and the world around us, and our behaviors follow suit, resulting in self-hatred and ultimately perpetuating the cycle to begin again.

Breaking Unhealthy Cycles

By understanding someone's past, current condition, and repetitive thoughts or behaviors, you can usually begin to map out a cycle. Once a negative cycle is identified, it's important to implement tools that will turn a negative cycle into a positive one. The first step in breaking a destructive cycle is to begin to create a positive environment. From there, if the client learns how to manage their relationship with God, self-talk, needs, and boundaries, their view of themselves will begin to change dramatically.

Not all cycles are the same, so the important piece to grasp here is that when you recognize that someone is perpetually "going around the mountain," stop and figure out what is fueling it! If you go after the low expectations, for example, before addressing their negative self-image, you're wasting time.

Here are a few keys for you to keep in mind as you help people identify their unhealthy cycles:

- **Use a whiteboard to map out their cycle.** This is beneficial for a few reasons:

  ◦ You can verify that you and your client are on the same page

  ◦ The client can gain a visual understanding of their patterns

- **Practice declarations and positive self-talk.** If people live in a negative cycle, chances are their self-talk is negative, at least in this area of their life. Encourage your client to practice positive self-talk and declare, out loud, the opposite of their negative beliefs.

- **Make a "beliefs map."** Similar to creating a plan for getting beyond trigger points, a person can write out the progression of their beliefs and use this "map" to identify unhealthy beliefs and create a plan for moving forward. We will discuss this further in the "Working Through Pain" section of this workbook.

REFLECT

Scenario: A six-year-old and eight-year-old boy go fishing together. The six-year-old boy, who grew up in a positive environment, says, "When I go to college, I want to go to a college where there is a pond so I can fish." The eight-year-old boy, who grew up in a negative environment, nods and says, "That sounds nice. I love fishing with you. Maybe I can come visit you then?"

What belief systems already exist in these two young boys based on the small amount of information given?

_____

_____

_____

_____

Closing Keys

Every person operates within a specific and unique belief system. Identifying belief systems is an important part of the process when trying to determine the root causes of problems that our clients are experiencing. Belief systems perpetuate cycles of thoughts and behaviors, which are traps if the belief systems are negative and unhealthy. People often talk about "going around the same mountain" time and time again, and when that's the case, we know that there is some sort of unhealthy cycle stemming from an unhealthy belief system.

Lesson Four

ROOT ISSUES

Identifying and Exposing Root Issues

It is essential that you persevere to discover the root cause of every problem. Negative root issues are found on the heart-level in the places where unhealthy belief systems and cycles originate. Issues that originate in the heart will manifest themselves in our thoughts and behaviors, which Jesus explains to us in the Bible:

> *The [intrinsically] good man produces what is good and honorable and moral out of the good treasure [stored] in his heart; and the [intrinsically] evil man produces what is wicked and depraved out of the evil [in his heart]; for his mouth speaks from the overflow of his heart. (Luke 6:45, Amplified Bible)*

If someone is in a cycle of drug addiction, the drug addiction stems from a root cause, and the addiction cannot be cut off until the root issue is discovered and disempowered. Simply put, if you cut the root, you will kill the fruit.

In the Old Testament, God appointed Jeremiah to stand up against kingdoms, some of which he was told to "uproot and tear down," and others which he was told to "build and plant."[1] If our struggle is not against flesh and blood but against the authorities and powers of the unseen world, we too have the same call as Jeremiah.[2] God promises that "not a root or branch will be left" when he eradicates evil for good.[3] When we come alongside God in this process, we join in God's redemptive work to bring healing by removing the root of the problem.

> *Keep your heart with all diligence, for out of it spring the issues of life. (Proverbs 4:23, NKJV)*

---

1 See Jeremiah 1:10 of the *New Living Translation.*

2 See Ephesians 6:12.

3 See Malachi 4:1 of the *New Century Version.*

Search Beyond the Symptoms

When you go to the doctor because you're feeling unwell, you want two questions answered: What is wrong with me, and what do I need to do to be well? For a doctor to successfully treat a sick patient, they need to determine the cause of the symptoms in order to get to the root of the problem. The same goes for an emotional health counselor. Examples of external symptoms that point to a root issue include:

- Anxiety

- Addiction

- Anger

- Depression

- Marital Distress

- Financial Distress

- Strained Relationships

Sometimes making a diagnosis is simple, but other times it requires blood work, CAT scans, or an MRI. While it might be inconvenient, a person who is feeling really sick or experiencing a lot of pain is typically willing to undergo any test in order to get to the root that is causing the problem. We must be willing to relentlessly pursue emotional and spiritual health just as we would pursue health in our physical bodies.

REFLECT

Besides the common external symptoms listed in the section above, what are some other symptoms that you've observed in people you've worked with that point to deeper root issues?

_____

_____

_____

_____

_____

Root Issue Detours

You cannot fix a physical heart problem with a Band-Aid, and bandages don't work for emotional heart problems either. Because "heart surgery" can feel scary and vulnerable, it's not uncommon for people to try to take detours rather than approach the problem head-on. As the counselor, you should be aware of these frequently-traveled detours because often they actually lead people around a mountain and back to where they began, no healthier.

- **The "Try Harder" Detour**

  Many people skip over the heart issue (root) and try to attack the symptoms (behaviors) first. While techniques such as Cognitive Behavioral Therapy are helpful, they only truly take effect once the heart issues have been exposed and uprooted. Yes, to "try harder next time" is a noble plan, but it won't yield different results without addressing the root issue of the problem. People who want to "try harder next time" usually don't accomplish their goals, which feels defeating and leads to hopelessness. If you're working with a client who wants to "try harder" rather than address the source of the problem, you might hear them say things like:

  - "No matter how hard I try, I never succeed."

  - "I won't ever be able to change."

  - "I've been here so many times before."

- **The "Quick Fix" Detour**

  Oftentimes when people discover they have a problem, their first response is to search out every book, sermon, and blog under the sun and thoroughly research the issue, hoping that they can attain freedom by learning about the issue. People usually want a self-help manual that outlines a three-step formula to help them achieve their desired outcome, and while this may work sometimes, it is not a universal solution. More often than not, sustained success is attained when we choose to become vulnerable in our quest for health. This means that instead of trying to solve a problem on your own with a formula, you enlist the strength of your community. Long-term solutions come as we allow others to walk with us, give input, and keep us accountable for growth. If you're working with a client who wants a quick fix, they may use "maybe" statements that keep them isolated, constantly searching for something better.

- *Maybe if I read that book that helped my friend, I'll get some breakthrough.*

- *Maybe if I go to all those emotional health classes, I'll figure out what's wrong.*

- *I bought this latest sermon series to help me understand my problem, and maybe this will finally help.*

- *Maybe I just need prayer.*

If we are not careful in the counseling process, we will focus more on the symptoms and miss the roots, which stem from the heart. People become so aware of the external problems that they start with what they can easily see. Others are terrified to face their hearts and will do anything to avoid pain. As a counselor, your objective is to help people get to the root of their heart issue so they have the opportunity to get well.

REFLECT

Scenario: While shopping at the grocery store the other day, Marcus found himself staring at and sexualizing a woman in the checkout line. Feeling guilt and shame about his sin and the recurring struggle, he determines to work on his self-control. In his well-meaning attempt to "take every thought captive," he fails again and wonders why he can't seem to find breakthrough.[4]

Explain why Marcus isn't getting the breakthrough he so desires. What are some possible root issues that might be at play?

_____

_____

_____

_____

_____

---

4 See 2 Corinthians 10:5 of the English Standard Version.

EMOTIONAL PROSPERITY

Factors Leading to Root Issues

Cultural backgrounds, past traumas, and difficult relationships are a few examples of factors that could be at play in the formation of root issues in people's hearts. When you're working with clients to show them how root issues are manifesting in their lives, make a list of the symptoms your client is experiencing. Then, using a chart like the one below, ask questions around these topics to find out which of these factors could be causing the root issues of their symptoms. Take notes and address each one as you work with your client. This is not an exhaustive list, so feel free to add to it!

SYMPTOMS	
Had an emotional affair	Inability to connect with spouse
Lies	Pornography addiction
Strained relationship with dad	Feels shame
Other:	*Other:*
Other:	*Other:*

POSSIBLE CONTRIBUTING FACTORS	NOTES
Family Background	*Dad was harsh and distant*
Cultural Background	
Present Stress	*Husband travels for work, baby at home, stress from guilt & shame*
Past or Present Trauma	*Past history of major sexual promiscuity*
Major Success/Failure	*Had an affair with a married man years ago*
Friendships	*Shallow*
Relationship with God	
Identity	*Doesn't feel lovable*

Tools for Finding Root Issues

While working with your clients to identify root issues, there are certain things to look out for that will help steer you in the right direction. Ultimately, the Holy Spirit inside them is the best counselor and guide, and He will be the best help in this process!

———

Recognizing Violations

Dictionary.com[5] defines *violate* like this:

> **violate**
>
> verb (used with object)
>
> 1. to break, infringe, or transgress (a law, rule, agreement, promise, instructions, etc.).
>
> 2. to break in upon or disturb rudely; interfere thoughtlessly with: *to violate his privacy.*
>
> 3. to break through or pass by force or without right: *to violate a frontier.*
>
> 4. to treat irreverently or disrespectfully; desecrate; profane: *violate a human right.*
>
> 5. to molest sexually, especially to rape.

Anytime a person afflicts someone with something against their will, and anytime a person acts contrary to their *own* personal convictions, they've committed a violation. Violations can be inflicted or self-imposed, and I would add these to the definition of a violation:

> 6. to inflict upon someone anything outside of God's will for a person.
>
> 7. to stray away from a personal conviction (James 4:17).

Without self-awareness, people won't necessarily know that they've violated themselves or another person because the thoughts and feelings that lead to violations are often subconscious. Self-awareness is the ability to know what is going on inside of you at all times. When people learn how to be self-aware, they are then able to catch themselves before the violation occurs.

———

5 Violate. (n.d.). Retrieved from http://www.dictionary.com/

A person who is not aware that he is doing anything wrong
has no desire to be put right. You have to catch yourself
doing it before you can reform.

SENECA

A violation is an indicator that there is a root issue at play, and a good first step in recognizing the cause of the problem is to ask your client what they were thinking or feeling right before they violated themselves or another person.

Here are a few questions you could ask to determine what the root issue behind the violation may be:

- What usually happens just before you choose this destructive behavior? Do you recognize any patterns?

- Why do you think you chose that behavior when you knew it would violate your conscience?

- Did making this choice happen as a result of something unrelated in order to feel in control or powerful?

Recognizing Red Flags

Understanding red flags is very important when dealing with violations and root issues. Anytime a need goes unmet, it will always lead to pain. Red flags are warning signs that pain is present and requires attention. Like small sparks in a dry forest, red flags are weak spots in the walls of a person's heart, eventually giving way to destruction if not dealt with quickly. These flags can be physical, emotional or spiritual in nature. For example, feeling tired, lonely, or hopeless are all indicators that something requires attention internally. When a person knows their weaknesses, they are much more prepared to recognize their red flags and extinguish the spark before it becomes a flame. Teaching people how to get their needs met in a healthy way starts with helping them recognize their red flags.

Knowing your red flags helps you understand yourself and stay away from the shame or self-judgment that comes from violating yourself or another person. A person's red flag indicates, *"You have an unmet need!"* In counseling, you can help a person establish boundaries that account for their triggers ahead of time.

Ted Bundy, for example, is one of the most infamous criminals in American history. People know him as a cold-blooded killer, but he didn't start out as a monster. At the age of thirteen, Ted Bundy got addicted to pornography. His addiction to soft porn dramatically increased as the years went on until he craved more explicit and violent forms of pornography, eventually leading him to commit heinous crimes.[6] Those violations began as small sparks that, when left unattended, grew into a forest fire.

I realize this story is an extremely dramatic example of what can happen when red flags aren't caught, but the truth is that if Ted Bundy would have taken care of the need he had in his heart at the age of 13 when it was just a spark, his life would not have taken the course it did. Because he failed to meet his valid needs in a healthy way (likely intimacy, connection, escape, or something else that most of us can relate to), that small spark of perversion grew into a costly rage. As counselors, we want our clients to leave a session with all the tools they need to address root issues by recognizing violations and learning to take care of their own sparks before they turn into fires.

———

1+2 Always Equals 3

When listening to a client's story, make note of anything that doesn't "add up" or anything that seems "off" to you. Then ask questions around those topics to get to the root issue. Before you can "fix" any problem, you have to be able to identify the issue, and identifying the root can be a challenge if you don't know what to look for. If someone explains their symptoms, past, current belief systems, and triggers, we should be able to take that information and logically tell them how they got where they are. In a world where people are prone to think their problem is chemical or spiritual, using simple logic simplifies counseling. Most of the time, a person's life does add up, because every action has a reaction.

———

6 Casuso, J. (1989, January 24). Bundy Blames Pornography. *The Chicago Tribune.* Retrieved from http://www.chicagotribune.com/

REFLECT

Scenario: For the last three years, Maria has been hiding a secret bank account from her husband, Jordan. When Jordan found out about it and confronted Maria, she said she didn't see anything wrong with it because it's money she made all on her own. They come to you for help.

Considering that 1+2=3, what doesn't "add up" in this scenario?

_____

_____

_____

_____

What questions would you ask Maria to figure out her root issues?

_____

_____

_____

_____

Scenario: In this same session, Jordan admits to hiding financial statements from Marie because he has been afraid that she would spend their money unwisely if she knew how much they had.

How do you know that Jordan is violating his conscience, and what need would you suppose he has that is causing him to violate himself and his marriage?

_____

_____

_____

_____

What red-flags would you suggest that Maria and Jordan look out for, respectively?

_____

_____

_____

_____

Blessed are those who find Wisdom and
those who gain understanding.

PROVERBS 3:13, NIV

Closing Keys

To help people get breakthrough, counselors have to be able to identify root issues beneath a myriad of symptomatic problems. People often find it challenging to face problems head-on, and some will try to take the "easy road," but the truth is that there's no way to a solution without addressing the real issues at hand. Being able to recognize violations and red flags will be key in leading people to a place where they can see their root issues for themselves, thus empowering them to change.

NOTES

SECTION TWO

—

Solve

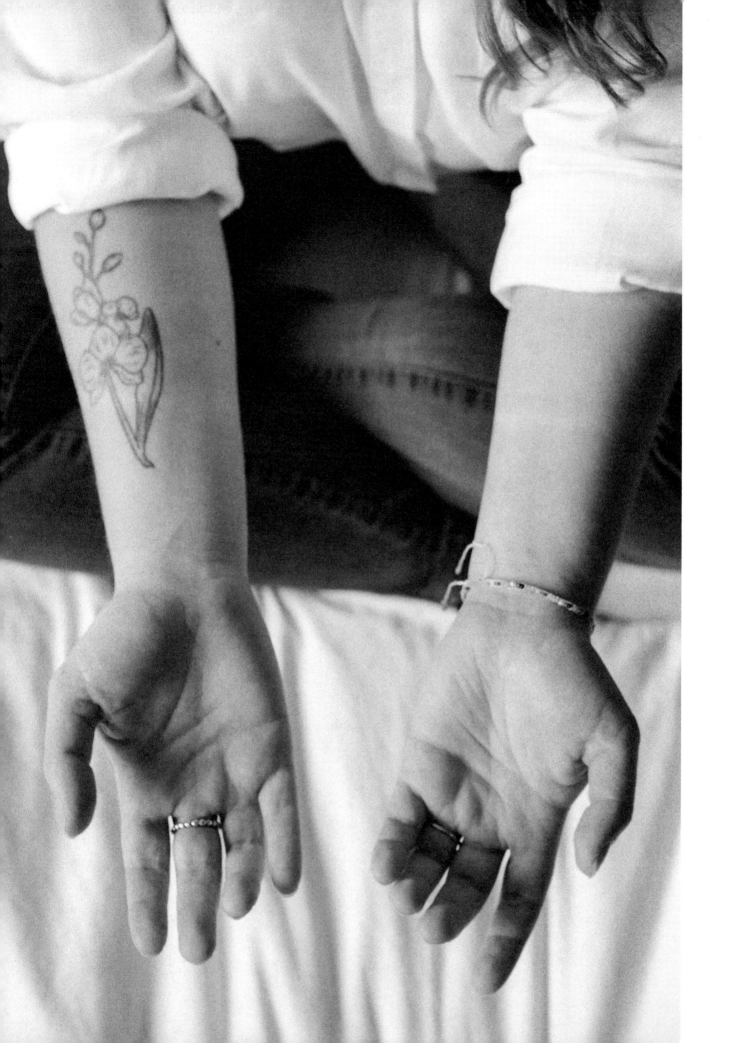

Lesson Five

REPENTANCE

Learning to Solve Problems

Now that you know how to prepare for and begin counseling appointments, and now that you know how to identify cycles, belief systems, and root issues, we can talk about the process of solving an issue. It is essential to remember that as a counselor, your job is to aid in the healing process by asking good questions, introducing helpful tools, and leading someone to the opportunity to get breakthrough. It is not your responsibility to make a client dependent upon you in order to walk in freedom.

> *You cannot help someone who doesn't have a problem, and you cannot work harder on someone else's problem than they do. –Danny Silk*

If you know anything about baking cakes, you know that most cakes have certain basic ingredients in common including flour, sugar, baking powder, salt, and butter. Depending on the type of cake you're baking, you use varying amounts of these basic ingredients, as well as adding anything else you need to yield your desired outcome. Similarly, in counseling, in order to yield the desired result of health and freedom for a client, there are some basic ingredients that you'll need in varying measure. Once a root issue or target is identified, you'll need to walk your client through these three foundational processes, with varying emphases, according to the specific situation:

- Repentance
- Working Through Pain
- Forgiveness

As counselors, we guide people through these processes in order to break unhealthy cycles and restore each person to God's original design.

It's important to take your time while working through each process to ensure your clients get the freedom that each one provides. Skipping necessary steps can leave people hurting and broken, making it exceptionally harder to help them get free later on. The more times people pursue breakthrough unsuccessfully, the more hopeless they become.

In this lesson, we will specifically cover the process of Repentance, and in Lessons 6 & 7, Working through Pain and Forgiveness, respectively.

Repentance

In counseling, there are beautiful and sobering moments that we get to share with our clients when they recognize and understand, for the first time, the root issues driving their unhealthy cycles of bondage. People often feel a sense of remorse over the reality of their dysfunction when they recognize the root of their problem, but repentance is more than deep remorse. It's so much more than saying, "I'm sorry." We want people to feel *empowered,* not just remorseful because understanding the root of a problem is a powerful position in that adjustments can be made when ownership is assumed!

The truth is, "I'm sorry" doesn't cut it! True biblical repentance is actually best defined as a changing of one's mind. It can be translated this way: *To turn around and go the other direction; to change the way one thinks.*[1]

A lot of people go wrong in thinking that repentance is a moment or an experience of deep regret and conviction. In reality, it's more than that! True repentance is actually a process because changing the way you think and behave after years of unhealthy habits doesn't typically happen overnight.

Why is changing the way you think so hard?

In the early stages of your life, the way you think and process information is developed as a result of your family culture, experiences, and other environmental factors. Years of subconscious, repetitive thought patterns create literal grooves in your brain that act like well-traveled highways for information. These highways of unhealthy subconscious thinking require *conscious* effort to reroute or remove. Simply put, changing the way you think is hard work!

------

1 Strong's Concordance: 3340.metanoèo. (n.d.). Retrieved from http://biblehub.com/. See also Romans 12:2.

I find neuroscience to be absolutely fascinating, and there are many good resources available to you if you want to understand it better, but for the sake of simplicity, consider your brain and body as a sophisticated communication network. There are all kinds of messages sent and received many times per second, most of which are transmitted entirely subconsciously. This vast flow of information about your wants, needs, and desires determines your physical and emotional behaviors. Let's look at a couple of the dynamics of this powerful communication network.

- **Thoughts catalyze actions.** According to Dr. Athena Staik, "Your thoughts create inner standards or rules that spark neurochemical dynamic processes, which selectively govern your choices and actions with precision. It takes a thought to spark an emotion, or drive a decision to take an action, or to take no action at all. And emotions give meaning to thoughts; they are the spark."[2]

- **Bad thoughts create more bad thoughts.** Dr. Staik says that toxic thinking "stimulates the body's reward or learning centers with pseudo feel-good feelings. It also activates the body's fear response, which further increases the likelihood that the defensive behaviors it triggers will be repeated."[3] This sheds light on why we perpetuate negative thinking, even when we don't want to!

- **Thought patterns are learned and can, therefore, be unlearned.** Every person's brain interprets the world differently, but our interpretations are not permanent because they are based on thoughts that can be unlearned, changed, or replaced.

By definition, repentance requires changing the way you think, and neuroscientifically, that means you literally have to reshape the patterned grooves in your brain. This typically requires time and intentionality. Of course, it is possible for God to supernaturally and instantaneously intervene, but more often than not, true repentance is a process.

> *As a single footstep will not make a path on the earth, so a single thought*
> *will not make a pathway in the mind. To make a deep physical path, we*
> *walk again and again. To make a deep mental path, we must think over*
> *and over the kind of thoughts we wish to dominate our lives.*
>
> **HENRY DAVID THOREAU**

2 Staik, A. (2016). The Neuroscience of Changing Toxic Thinking Patterns (1 of 2). *Psych Central.* Retrieved from https://blogs.psychcentral.com/
3 Staik, A. (2016). Toxic Thinking Patterns – How Pseudo "Feel-Goods" Put Your Brain on Hold. *Psych Central.*
Retrieved from https://blogs.psychcentral.com/

REFLECT

Scenario: Ella is struggling to find acceptance at school. At seventeen years old, she feels like a failure because she cannot make good friends. She mentions to you that she cannot remember a time when she had friends or knew how to connect with other kids. Through inquiring about her background, you find that she comes from a home with parents who work a lot and often leave her by herself. She tells you, "I will never be like the other kids in class. I will always be an outcast. Life isn't even worth living." Together, you've discovered that the root cause of her pain is that she doesn't believe she is lovable.

If true repentance requires that Ella "changes her mind," what are some of the thought processes that you can identify that need to change in order for Ella to walk the other way in the truth that she truly IS lovable?

_____

_____

_____

_____

_____

The Process of Repentance

As we've already discussed, you cannot change the way you think in a minute or even a day. Scientifically, it takes a minimum of twenty-one days to break a habit and even longer to create a new one![4]

If you want to travel from California to Texas, you would have to prepare for the journey and acknowledge the fact that you'll have to take a different route than you'd take to the grocery store or work like you do in your normal routines. Simply _wanting_ to arrive in Texas is not enough to get you there. Similarly, in order to gain new ground in a process of internal breakthrough, people

---

4 Taylor, R. (2017). New Habits For Old. In _Willpower: Discover It, Use It and Get What You Want._ Hoboken: Wiley.

EMOTIONAL PROSPERITY

need to gain understanding, create a strategy, and execute a plan! True repentance is largely the commitment to do whatever it takes, for however long it takes, to break old habits and mindsets and replace them with Heaven's Truth.

The first step in the process of repentance is letting your heart feel the conviction of not having been aligned with God's truth over your life. The remorse, conviction, and beautiful exchange of honest apology to God is a significant part of the process! Remember, we can't fix a problem that "doesn't exist." But this is just the beginning! The second step in the process of repentance is actually recognizing that you cannot keep the same belief system and expect different results. Thirdly, you must renounce the old lies and replace them with truth to set yourself on a new path towards your destination of health. This process of renunciation is simple, but we will discuss if briefly to ensure your understanding.

———

Renunciation

According to *dictionary.com,* "renunciation" can be understood as "an act or instance of relinquishing, abandoning, repudiating, or sacrificing something, as a right, title, person, or ambition; to speak the opposite."[5]

There are many times when people have a wrong belief system holding them hostage, simply because of how integrated it has become in their everyday lives. In these scenarios, intentional effort will be required in order for lasting change to take root. Renunciation is one of the key ingredients to breaking these cycles, and it does not have to be long and drawn out. Following a few simple steps can take a client further down the road to freedom. Let's explore the steps in the context of Lukas's scenario.

———

5 Renunciation. (n.d.). *Dictionary.com Unabridged.* Retrieved from http://www.dictionary.com/

REFLECT

Scenario: Lukas is afraid of getting to know people, and even more so for people to know him. He shows anti-social behaviors and cannot connect to his peers because of anxiety. While at work, Lukas often gets ridiculed for his lack of social awareness, which only furthers his anxiety and antisocial behaviors. As you can probably tell, Lukas often feels misunderstood and is losing hope daily about life getting any better. In a previous session, he began to work through the pain of an abusive father, experienced the emotions of disappointment, and forgave his father for not being available on a heart level. Now, the purpose of this appointment is to begin the breaking of negative thought patterns that were created in his childhood through renunciation.

Steps Involved in Renunciation:

1. **Pray and ask Holy Spirit to show the client what lies they are believing.** Lies are thoughts which don't line up with the Word of God that person believes and acts out.

   Lukas may believe that intimacy is scary; however, he doesn't have to stay trapped in this negative belief system. Identifying the lie that "intimacy is scary" begins the process.

2. **Identify the root of the lies and where they entered the life of your client.** Quite often people may come to realize they have a problem, but they might not know what the root is. We should ask Holy Spirit to guide us into all truth (John 16:13).

   If Lukas believes that intimacy is scary, have him ask Holy Spirit, "Holy Spirit, when did the lie that 'intimacy is scary' enter my life?" Give him time to hear from Holy Spirit and tell you what He says. Once Lukas finds out what the lie is and where it came from, it's now time for the Holy Spirit to let him know the truth. Lukas can simply ask "Holy Spirit, what is the truth about intimacy?" From there, Lukas is now able to take the next step.

3. **Replace the lies with the truth.** Once a lie is renounced, it is time to replace the lie with the truth. Often the truth is the opposite of the lie and should line up with Scripture.

   Lukas could say, "I receive the truth that intimacy is healthy and good."

Get Practical

There are many practical strategies that people can implement in their lives to aid in the process of repentance, renouncing lies, and forming new mindsets. These are tools people can use when they're tempted to revert back to their old beliefs and behaviors. These tools can also be used to proactively practice healthy mindsets. Here are a few I recommend the most often:

- **Use your mirror.** Writing truths on your bathroom mirror is a great way to remind yourself of the truth that opposes the toxic beliefs you are trying to repent from. It's not enough to recognize the lie! We must renounce the lie and replace it with the Word of God. Taking a dry erase marker to your mirror and covering it with healthy mindsets is a practical way to keep the Truth in front of you!

  Ex: If you're repenting from self-hatred, litter your mirror with phrases like this:

  - I am worth caring for!
  - I am beautifully and wonderfully made!
  - I am made in the image of God!

- **Set an alarm.** Setting the alarm on your cell phone or one in your home for different times throughout the day can remind you to stop and give attention to the steps you need to take.

  Ex: If you're repenting from relying on money to give you a sense of security and learning to trust the Lord as your provider, set an alarm that goes off five times a day to remind you to recall the times in your life when you've experienced the Lord's provision.

- **Ask an expert.** Chances are, if you knew what to do about your situation, you would have already done it! The best posture to take when walking through the process of repentance is that of a learner. Submit yourself to hearing from the best and commit to learn and grow in your areas of weakness! You can find experts on podcasts and TedTalks, in books, or with counselors. The main goal is to strategically form a team of "experts" that help you along in your journey of building a new culture of truth inside of you.

  For example, if you are repenting from the fear of being trapped or controlled in your marriage, see a marriage counselor that will give you wisdom, practical tools, and exercises to help you uproot the lies you have believed about this.

Old fears will pop up, but if you're proactively setting yourself up for success with tools like using your mirror, setting your alarms, and building a team of experts around you, you will be well on your way to creating healthy new habits.

Here is a list of questions your client should be able to answer before they leave your office when they are working through repentance:

- Do you feel like you have a good grasp on what the problem is and where repentance is needed?

- Are you clear on what you can do every day this week to proactively move forward?

- Who is on your team of "experts?"

The majority of positive change in people's lives
is the fruit of true repentance.

REFLECT: A COUNSELING STORY

I once met with a couple that needed marriage counseling, and they were the perfect example of two people having a victim mentality. As I listened to Jim share, he communicated that he felt that Sarah was nagging and impossible to please. According to Jim, Sarah had no respect for his boundaries, especially when their discussions turned into arguments. "She doesn't let me leave the room or give me any time to think! She just keeps hounding me," Jim complained. "Sarah is totally controlling!" Jim admitted that when provoked, he often punched holes in the wall and smashed things out of anger.

My first thought was "Wow! I'm so glad I'm not in this guy's shoes!" But after giving him time to vent, I started by asking Jim what had he previously done to work on his relationship with his wife.

There was a long pause accompanied with a sigh. "Um, I guess I'm here," he responded. "Okay," I said, "Did you set up this meeting or did Sarah?" (I already knew the answer to this question, but I really wanted Jim to see the answer for himself.) "Uh, she did," he admitted. Continuing down the same train of thought, I asked Jim, "What have you initiated in order to get some help in your marriage?"

REFLECT: A COUNSELING STORY *(continued)*

After thinking for a second, Jim responded, "I talk to my mom sometimes. Well, actually, my mom found out that we're having trouble because Sarah called her. She normally calls my parents when we are having a hard time."

As we continued talking, Jim's half of the problem became clear to me. Jim never talked to anyone about his marriage, including his best friend. To make matters worse, when I asked him what he normally does to get rid of the pain and frustration he feels, his response was, "I normally just try to forget about it." It didn't take a psychiatrist to figure out that Jim's plan of ignoring his frustration and stuffing his pain wasn't working!

"Jim, it doesn't seem like your plan has been working very well. What have you done to meet your wife's love languages?" I probed. Seemingly annoyed, Jim answered, "Even if I try, I don't ever seem to be able to meet them. It feels pretty impossible. I've been really frustrated lately trying to meet Sarah's needs. I feel hopeless."

I heard the frustration in his voice. "Jim, what are you going to do about your marriage?" I asked. "I don't know. I wish Sarah wasn't such a mess and so hard to live with," he responded. He believed that she was the sole problem in the relationship, and I knew that as long as his belief system remained, he would feel powerless to fix what was going on inside of him.

I responded back to Jim, "It doesn't feel like she is really the whole problem to me. You made her responsible to get help for your marriage. She is the one that contacted your parents and me. You haven't done anything proactive to work on your marriage other than the things that she hounds you about, and you have no process for dealing with the pain and frustration that you feel from not being successful. You still believe that she is the sole problem in this relationship. I'm not surprised that she nags you, Jim. It's the only way to motivate you in this relationship. You have empowered her to be your mother." I saw the light bulb exploding in his head, and for the first time, Jim realized that he had given his power away to his wife and that she had become responsible for the health of their marriage.

So many people want to be like Jim: completely un-responsible for the condition of their lives because it's so much easier if their problems are everyone else's fault. Jim had given up on his relationship. He had told his wife he was considering getting a divorce because she was making him miserable.

What Jim didn't realize until that day in my office was that if he spent less time worrying about what Sarah was going to do and more time trying to figure out what he was going to do, he could actually fix the majority of his own problems. Because Jim had never taken personal responsibility for his life or marriage, he was always frustrated and overwhelmed because his peace and happiness were at the mercy of his wife.

Once Jim realized that he had given all of his power away to Sarah, he was able to repent for his victim mentality and figure out practical steps toward regaining his power while loving his wife. To this day, Jim and Sarah are happy and thriving in their marriage!

Which unhealthy belief systems did Jim need to change in order to be powerful in his marriage?

_____

_____

_____

_____

_____

What practical things would you have Jim do on a daily basis in order to walk out repenting from each of the lies that he was believing?

_____

_____

_____

_____

_____

Closing Keys

True repentance is most often a process, and you know repentance has happened by the fruit of a changed life! When we are helping people walk through the process of repentance, it's important that we are able to give them tools for change and creative ideas as to how they can practically CHANGE the way they think. Leading them on the journey of rewriting their belief systems can be a challenge, but it's important to believe in your client's ability to overcome.

NOTES

_____
_____
_____
_____
_____
_____
_____
_____
_____
_____
_____
_____
_____
_____
_____
_____
_____
_____
_____
_____
_____

Lesson Six
WORKING THROUGH PAIN

Psychological studies rooted in Cognitive-Behavioral therapies are recognizing that Experiential Avoidance (the avoidance of thoughts, experiences, and memories that create pain or discomfort) is a bit of a Catch-22 in that, as a person strives to relieve themselves of in-the-moment pain, the more likely it is that the problem will persist.[1] But regardless of this fact, people spend countless quantities of time, money, and energy working to avoid pain in their lives.

As pastoral counselors, part of our job is to equip people with tools to work through pain in order to break its power and cyclical effect on the lives of people that Jesus died to free!

I want to start with a parable entitled "The Frozen Heart," which I wrote in The Supernatural Power of Forgiveness, because it illustrates how people get trapped in cycles of pain when their hearts are disconnected from its circumstances.[2] This allegory depicts many of the men and women you will counsel—people who have spent their entire lives never connecting to their emotions or working through pain. Throughout the excerpt, there are intermittent spaces for you to process the things that are revealed in the allegory.

---

1 Hayes, S. C., Wilson, K. G., Gifford, E. V., Follette, V. M., & Al, E. (1996). Experiential Avoidance and Behavioral Disorders: A Functional Dimensional Approach to Diagnosis and Treatment. *Journal of Consulting and Clinical Psychology, 64*(6), 1152-1168.

2 Vallotton, K., Vallotton, J., & Baker, H. (2014). *The Supernatural Power of Forgiveness.* Minneapolis, MN: Chosen Books.

The Frozen Heart

Take a walk with me down a long, slender corridor, a place where life has been forgotten. The hardened walls of ice carry no ability in themselves to feel or breathe, for they have been sealed shut from the light of day. As you pass through the corridor, you can see the work of many hands. Carved deep within the walls of ice are the scars of ancient history. Murals from top to bottom tell the stories of incessant abuse and perversion that have plagued this place.

As you continue down the frozen corridor, you come to a set of steel bars and are unable to go any further. Lying on the floor are thousands of words of affirmation and love, all of them worthless--shattered to pieces--while words of hate and rage claw at the door, trying to find their way into the cage. Peering through the steel bars, you see a heart torn and cold from the empty promises of affectionate deceit. Upon seeing the bleeding heart, you begin to beg and plead to be let in. At the top of your lungs you cry out for mercy, but your words only echo off the ice-laden walls. There is no one here to care, no one to hear your plea. Quickly, your pleading turns to torment as you frantically search for the keys that unlock this door, for it won't be long until this cold heart is frozen in time, unable to ever feel again.

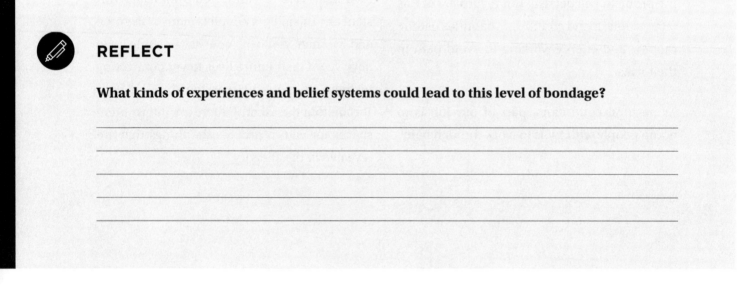

REFLECT

What kinds of experiences and belief systems could lead to this level of bondage?

_____

_____

_____

_____

_____

Digging through the shattered words, your fingers begin to bleed, but it matters not. For somewhere among the wreckage there must lie a key... a way in. You dig and dig until the concrete floor meets your bleeding fingers, but still there is no way in. In your frustration you scream at the heart, "Who put you here? Who would leave you here to rot in this frozen grave?" Your words carry through the bars, sinking compassion deep into the freezing heart. At your words he moans aloud, for he only hears the torment of past love. Without notice, the prison bars grow thicker, and the temperature drops in the corridor. Quickly you realize that the heart was the one that built this prison. No longer can it allow itself to unlock the steel cage that took so long to fortify. No longer can he risk the torment of hope deferred and love abused...

REFLECT

This revelation is often a powerful and painful one for people to experience. What are some of the possible effects of this unveiling of truth?

_____

_____

_____

_____

Looking through the ice, you begin to realize that your whole life was a horror of memories, a testimony of what happens to a heart that is left open to feel. Somewhere down the line, life became a routine of slowly shutting down. After all, one doesn't have to feel in order to live, especially when feeling is worse than dying. The tears try to run, but you're too cold; you're trapped inside yourself, inside the fortress you made. Running back to the heart, you pound on the cage screaming to be let in. "Can't you see we're going to die down here?" The heart groans at your words, but he's unwilling to move.

Falling to your knees, you begin to plead with him, recalling back to him your childhood. "I was there when love was abused, when all you wanted was the touch of a father. I was there when perversion became the comfort for a broken spirit, the only way out. I saw the pain in shutting down, knowing that it meant losing the possibility to ever bond again. And I see the hatred that you have toward me for not being able to protect you, for not being able to see through the deceptive lies."

REFLECT

Why is it important that this kind of real conversation be allowed to happen in a safe place with a client?

_____

_____

_____

_____

_____

For the first time in ages, the heart begins to cry at the realization that there's someone who knows, someone who sees where he's been. For even though the heart lives inside of a man, he is very much his own person needing to be explored and understood. The tears pour and the ice slowly melts as the heart begins to feel again. Never before has the heart felt protected enough to unlock the steel cage, but one by one, the bolts begin to break as promises are made. "I promise to love you more than anyone else. I promise to find a way to protect you. I promise to not be afraid to feel even when it hurts. And I promise to never disconnect from you again, leaving you alone to fend for yourself!"

Leaving the corridor that day, the only thing that is going to change inside of you is the decision to be powerful, to not hide anymore. Many of us have spent our whole lives not realizing what our heart is really needing, or even being aware of the punishment that life has dished out. Without the ability to connect to your heart, you have no way of really meeting your deepest needs. This type of living leaves people desperate for a way to cope with the onslaught of normal life because a need unmet leads to pain!

EMOTIONAL PROSPERITY

What steps could you take at this point to help a client move forward in the process of repentance as we discussed in Lesson 5?

_____

_____

_____

_____

_____

———

Valuing Emotions

No one sets out with the intent of locking themselves up inside a prison of ice. After all, who wants to be alone and unknown? The process of emotionally shutting down is our soul's last-ditch effort at surviving what it deems traumatic. When the pain fails to subside, your heart has to make a decision: go completely insane or disconnect from emotional reality.

Childhood upbringing is the most common place of pain I've found in people who are emotionally shut down. People are at their most vulnerable state as young children because they are powerless to change their circumstances. Kids often become victims of their parents' dysfunction, and they learn lessons about love and vulnerability that teach them to hide at all costs. For example, when the character in the allegory above looked back at his childhood and realized he was never really loved and cared for, he began to understand, for the first time, why his heart had locked itself up in the steel cage. Because the decision to hide and avoid pain usually happens at a young age, it's really common for adults to be unaware of what is actually happening.

There are countless ways that people protect themselves from having to take risks, keep themselves from feeling emotions, and compensate for the pain in their lives. But the important thing to realize is that God designed us to have feelings, and He is with us as we explore them. When God created man, He created in him a masterpiece of emotions. Here are some important things to consider:

- **Emotions are motivators.** Emotions are meant to excite us to action and actually help us get things done! Emotions stimulate our brains to tell our muscles to tense or relax, motivating us or de-motivating us to act. Without emotions, we wouldn't accomplish much!

- **Emotions assist in decision-making.** For example, when you think about doing something that contradicts your core values, your emotions will let you know that it's probably not a good idea based on the way that you *feel*. Even imagining a scenario will trigger your emotions and let you know if it feels like a good idea or not.

- **Emotions create strong bonds of connectivity and harmony between you and your environment.** I can't count how many times I've talked with kids who are completely heartbroken over the fact that their parents have never said the words "I love you" to them. Even as adults, the pain of living your whole life without having your parents ever emotionally connected to you is incredibly damaging. On the other hand, if you look back at some of the best times in your life with your friends or family, it was probably a time when you felt really emotionally connected. On the most fundamental level, we are created to connect to the world around us on a heart-to-heart level.

- **Emotions help us survive and thrive!** Negative emotions signal warnings and prompt us to act by running away, avoiding, or even fighting back. Positive emotions are so important that they actually boost your immune system, promote good self-esteem, and ward off depression.

God created both positive and negative emotions. There have been entire studies done on this subject! The important thing to understand is that it was God's original intent that we would live connected to our hearts. Checking in with our hearts each day to find out what's going on inside of us is a practical way to validate our emotions and become consciously aware of how we are doing. Here are some questions that someone can ask their heart in order to practice giving it a voice and identifying the places that need attention:

- How do I feel today?

- Why do I feel the way that I do?

- Heart, what do you need in order to be okay?

- What can I do about it?

If your emotional abilities aren't in hand, if you don't have self-awareness,
if you are not able to manage your distressing emotions, if you can't have
empathy and have effective relationships, then no matter how smart
you are, you are not going to get very far.

DANIEL GOLEMAN

Mourning Leads to Comfort

Most of the time, pain causes us to feel so incredibly powerless and hopeless that focusing on it seems to make it worse. The typical response to pain is to stuff it down or ignore it. However, without the process of mourning, there is no comfort! Mourning is a significant process on the road to wholeness! It is necessary, but because people are averse to addressing their pain, they typically rob themselves of this powerful experience.

Blessed are those who mourn, for they will be comforted.

MATTHEW 5:4, NIV

Mourning is the process by which people receive the real comfort they so need and desire, but because addressing the pain has to happen in order to mourn it, people often short-circuit their process, which leads them back around their mountain, feeding the pain cycles in their lives.

Processing Pain

Many people you see in your counseling office will not know how to deal with their pain in a thorough and healthy way, but before you begin the process of leading someone to address their places of mourning and pain, you will want to consider a few important things. Not every person will respond or react to the process the same way, so it's important to inform them that there is no cookie-cutter way to navigate through this time. Your clients will experience a range of emotions depending on their levels of pain, their personality types, and the circumstances they've walked through. As a counselor, be ready for this and give your client enough information that they don't feel confused or scared because you didn't communicate well. Here are some things to remember:

- Working through pain uncorks a person. Like a bottle that has been corked up and shaken for years, a person may be afraid that they'll explode if they open up. Make sure that your client knows what to do when they feel undone. For example, it may be helpful for them to process their emotions through journaling or talking with a really safe friend so they don't get too overwhelmed. Having a plan and a good support team is vital when processing pain.

- Painful thoughts are a gift. They should be allowed to come so that they can be validated and dealt with in a healthy way. Work through each painful thought or memory, one at a time, and give it permission to make you feel deeply. It's in the embracing of the pain, mourning the loss that took place, and asking for the Holy Spirit to come that a person can receive real comfort and God's truth about the pain. It's important to note that working through pain and dealing with unforgiveness go hand in hand. In the next lesson, we will go through this process step-by-step.

- Crying is a good thing. Crying is the body's instinctive way of purging negative emotions. To deny yourself the gratification of tears is to invalidate the emotions and hide the truth about how you feel. I always encourage people to go to a quiet place, to process through thoughts by crying, and writing and asking God what He thinks. After literally crying it out, pain subsides and the thoughts that were once painful don't hurt like they used to.

- Be wise about processing pain. It is not a good idea for a person to process when they are emotionally drained. This can lead to depression, anxiety, hopelessness, and other challenging things. One of the most important ingredients in processing pain is fun. When people have fun, they emotionally reset and recharge, making it possible to process more without burning out.

- Emotional health is linked to physical health. When processing through pain, a person should be exercising, eating well, sleeping well, and recharging on a daily basis. This will help them to work through the process in a safe manner without hitting extreme highs and lows.

Once people learn how to deal with pain instead of avoiding it, they are able to live a free life because they are not afraid of it anymore. When we successfully navigate through pain, we gain confidence to confront the old fears that once held us bound.

REFLECT: A COUNSELING STORY

I once counseled a woman who said that she never cried and had a hard time expressing her needs. She looked like Superwoman to those around her; she always attended to everybody else's needs and worked to make people feel loved and accepted, but she had a really hard time opening up about her own heart.

At her first appointment with me, Megan told me her story. Her father died when she was very young, which left her with an incredible amount of pain as a child. As if that wasn't hard enough, in Megan's teens her mother died in a fatal automobile accident. In a split second, she went from making plans to hang out with her mom to being alone in the world with no parents at all.

Shortly after her mother died, her friends and family gathered together to attend the funeral. Kind words were said and beautiful songs were sung, and then it was over. In an attempt to comfort Megan and celebrate the life of her mother, her friends hosted a time of worship and praise after the funeral. They felt like Megan needed to start a new chapter in her life and worship her way out of this terrible time!

As I listened to Megan that day, I realize that she had never allowed herself to mourn the loss of her parents, and because she never allowed herself to mourn, she was never able to get free from the pain. Megan's friends had great intentions! They wanted her to feel peace and joy in praise during a hard time! What none of them realized is that if you don't grieve and work through the pain, the pain never goes away.

Until that day in my office, Megan never allowed herself to access all of her heart because she believed that if she unlocked the hurting part of her heart, the pain would be too much to handle. She was trapped inside a façade of seeming joyful when, in fact, her heart was screaming for someone to acknowledge the pain that it was in. Only allowing yourself to feel joy is as dysfunctional as only allowing yourself to feel pain.

Megan and I spent a large portion of our time in that counseling appointment facing the reality that her mom and dad were never going to come back. I had her do things like write letters to her mom about how she felt the day she died and journal about how it felt to get that horrible phone call. Megan learned that she was not alone in her pain, but that God had answers for her and knew

REFLECT: A COUNSELING STORY *(continued)*

what she needed! Over time, through processing her reality and connecting to her heart, she was able to unlock her tears and face the reality that she so dreaded. To this day, Megan is free from the bondage of unprocessed pain!

For someone like Megan who spent a decade of her life ignoring her pain and devaluing negative emotions, what practical things would you have her do in order to practice giving her heart a voice and staying connected to her emotions?

_____

_____

_____

_____

_____

Closing Keys

Despite the aversion most people have to pain, life is inevitably painful at times. God created us with a beautiful array of emotions, positive and negative, that are valuable in helping us connect our heads and our hearts with our actions. The journey to wholeness includes a process of acknowledging and working through pain in a way that empowers the Holy Spirit to be our comforter and restorer. To avoid pain and the memories or thoughts that stir up pain is to deprive oneself of a healing process that is required for wholeness! Leading people through a process of working through pain is one of the most important things you will do as a pastoral counselor in helping people walk in freedom.

NOTES

Lesson Seven
FORGIVENESS

In my opinion, forgiveness is one of the most misunderstood and misused tools in the Kingdom. I have met hundreds of people who have spent years trying to forgive someone for something that happened long ago! Despite their genuine efforts and good hearts, they've misapplied the tool of forgiveness and therefore have not yet reaped the fruit of freedom. Forgiving someone for something does not mean that I have to feel great about what happened or that I have to reconcile with the violating party. Forgiving someone means that I give God permission to get justice on my behalf, and I release the other person from my judgments and myself from the responsibility to get justice through punishment. Most believers would agree that the above statement is true, but whether or not forgiveness is actually effective in your life will depend on how you apply it.

―

Understanding Forgiveness

In the Christian world, it's often taught that "forgiveness" is a simple formula or religious obligation. When this happens, forgiveness is reduced from a transformational tool to a form without power. Take, for example, a woman who has been raped. We would all probably agree that at some point she must forgive the one who raped her so that hatred and bitterness wouldn't eat her from the inside out. However, the truth is this: if she extends forgiveness before she acknowledges the pain and trauma, mourns her loss, and receives comfort from the Lord, she will most likely not experience the actual relief that she is supposed to gain from releasing someone from bondage.

The desire to forgive a perpetrator shouldn't stem from the threat of torment or punishment. It should originate from a place of compassion because forgiveness that comes out of compassion is genuine and true. Jesus is our model!

When Jesus took the weight of the world's sin upon Himself at the crucifixion, He experienced separation from God for the first time. Jesus felt the full weight of your sin and the full effects that sin has upon us. He felt the agony and torment of being separated from His Father and cried out in anguish, "My God, my God, why have you forsaken me?" (Matt. 27:46, New International Version). When Jesus took your sin and *chose* to forgive you, He was fully aware of how it felt and what it cost, but even when he was offered something to numb the pain, He refused to die unconscious of the pain involved in sacrificing Himself.

It's my opinion that He wanted to be fully aware of what he was doing. It says in Matthew 27:34, "They gave him vinegar (wine) to drink mingled with gall: and when he had tasted [thereof], he would not drink." Jesus refused the gall, knowing it was a poison, as He did not want to die from poisoning, but by His shed blood. To become the supreme sacrifice for the sins of all mankind, His blood had to be shed. His death made atonement for our sins so we could be fully forgiven and fully reconciled to Him! Christ didn't just throw a blanket of forgiveness over the sins of the world and ignore the fact that He was hurt and crushed by them. He went to the cross "for the joy set before Him!"[1] Jesus knew that He was about to get the ultimate justice, and because He always works all things out for good for those who love Him and makes all things new, there is nothing man can take from you that our Father cannot redeem!

The hurt and the pain you feel and the cost of sin need to be acknowledged and mourned, regardless of whether or not it was your sin or the sin of another. *After* you acknowledge, mourn, and process the pain with the Holy Spirit, then forgiveness can be genuinely applied. If you try to forgive without acknowledging the wrong that took place, then you're not really forgiving, but rather trying for a quick fix. You can say, "I forgive you" but still carry around unforgiveness like a disease if you don't acknowledge, mourn, and process the pain before extending forgiveness.

Genuine forgiveness that comes out of a pure place of compassion releases people from bondage and is a HUGE key to people walking in freedom and wholeness. Forgiveness is a process that you DO NOT WANT TO SKIP. Be thorough in these steps and make sure to turn over every "rock." I spend a lot of time walking people through forgiveness and so will you. A client's process of walking through forgiveness may take several days or weeks, and it may come a little at a time. You need to teach clients how to be empowered through this process because often their issues won't get fixed in one session. If you know the session is not enough time to complete the forgiveness process, teach them how to do it on their own when they are home.

---

1 See Hebrews 12:2 of the *New International Version*.

EMOTIONAL PROSPERITY

REFLECT

Scenario: Franklin is a successful, young businessman in his late 20's. By society's standards, Franklin has made a good life for himself. He has a nice house, car, and is climbing the corporate ladder. However, in his personal life, Franklin constantly battles self-hatred and shame. He's aware of his negative self-talk, and he admits that his anger turns to rage in some instances, but the actual source of the problem is unknown. As you ask questions about Franklin's father, he mentions that by the time his father was Franklin's age, he already had twice the accomplishments and notoriety that Franklin is experiencing. He tells you about how his father pushed him to be better his whole life and that Franklin often feels like he should be more successful than he is. In your counseling appointment, you invite the Holy Spirit to speak to Franklin, and when He does, Franklin hears for the first time that God the Father is proud of him and that Jesus wants to carry the burden of performance for him in exchange for peace and rest in his true identity.

As Franklin reconciles his experience of life with God's truth, you recognize that Franklin needs to forgive himself and his earthly father. How would you coach Franklin to walk through the process of forgiveness?

_____

_____

_____

_____

_____

In the scenario above, Franklin doesn't love himself for the man the Lord has created him to be, and he is measuring his success based upon a standard that he cannot attain. Franklin wants to be someone else: his dad. Furthermore, it seems as though his father helped to create a cycle of shame by sending Franklin messages that sounded like, "You are not enough; you could be better!"

There are two main violations here to recognize:

1. Franklin's dad, who wants him to be "more," and

2. Franklin, who has agreed with his dad that he "should" be more.

Because we only have the grace to do what the Lord has given us to do, Franklin will never be content comparing himself to his father. In order to break this nasty cycle of self-hatred and shame, Franklin is going to need to discover who God created him to be, break the agreement that he is "not enough," forgiving himself *and* his Dad. However, if Franklin tries to release forgiveness without honoring the emotions and pain associated with these violations, he will neither reach a place of compassion nor be able to truly forgive himself or his father.

Blanket Forgiveness Prayers

Have you ever said a prayer like this or coached a new believer to say something similar? *"God, forgive me for everything I've ever done wrong. I forgive everyone for anything they ever did to me."* Now, just to make it really clear, I don't believe there is anything wrong with this prayer, and for many settings, it's very appropriate. I have personally seen drug addictions gone in seconds as well as years of unforgiveness wiped away through a powerful prayer like this.

The problem with this type of prayer comes into play when we rely *solely* on a one-time blanket prayer to solve situations involving years of unforgiveness and bitterness. When a person is desperate for breakthrough, they will oftentimes say or do *anything* in hopes of change, without understanding that the words "I forgive you" require a mindset shift and a change in actions in order for the breakthrough to take place. Therefore, when we are extending forgiveness, there should be a conscious connection to those words and the person(s) to which it's being directed. The actual power of forgiveness does not come from the words we say or how badly we want a breakthrough. The power of forgiveness lies in our ability to connect our belief system to the Lord's and to extend mercy and grace from that position.

People want a transformed life. If we don't give them a complete model, then we create an expectation that goes unmet, which leads to pain and hopelessness.

Embrace the Process

The process of true and complete forgiveness can be meticulous. People typically want to get free in a day, but unless a true miracle happens, most people will go through a journey to get to wholeness. It is important for clients to learn how to embrace every aspect of the process, starting with repentance, which leads to dealing with pain, which sets them up to release and receive *true* forgiveness.

The process of working through pain and extending forgiveness will depend on the person and their situation, but there are a few keys to note that will get you and your clients on the right path.

1. **Acknowledge the Pain.** Have your client start by acknowledging the pain they are experiencing and what is happening in their heart.

2. **Focus on One Thing.** Often times, after realizing the root issue of a problem, people become aware of countless areas in their lives that need to be processed. Because it's impossible to process everything at once, have them pick ONE thought, feeling, or memory to focus on. With this one thought, have your client welcome the emotions that come without filtering them. As discussed in Lesson 6, emotions are a part of God's design and a necessary and natural part of working through issues. We cannot afford to be afraid of people's emotions, nor do we want them to be afraid of their own. Your client will need to be fully honest about what they are feeling, thinking and experiencing in this step. This could look like journaling, talking through the pain, or anything else that will help to process what is going on inside.

3. **Find the Theme.** All of us have experienced a time when we have cried or written for so long that there is literally nothing left to say. Once your client has reached this point, help them find the theme or repeated question that needs to be resolved. For instance, "Am I lovable?" or "God, do you see me?" could be examples of an emerging theme. Once you have found this theme or question, have them take it to God.

4. **Take it to God.** Having God answer your client's true question is key to their healing because it is not the theory of God, but the words of God, which heal and bring life. Have them ask God what he thinks about the theme or question that emerged from the process. Engaging with God in the midst of vulnerability and emotional honesty will open the door for him to give his perspective. Once God has responded to the issues of the heart and your client has received hope, they will be able to see through God's eyes and connect to compassion for the person that caused the pain.

5. **Find Compassion & Forgive.** With the truth received from the Lord about their pain, have your client ask God how he sees the person who hurt them. This should open the door for them to feel compassion for that person. It's important to remember that forgiveness without compassion is often fruitless. When a person is connected to the heart of God for another, they are able to see the greater picture and are no longer in need of earthly justice. Forgiveness offered from this place is truly genuine. Once your client has reached a place of compassion, have them go through and apply forgiveness

for each offense that they needed to process. For example, "I forgive you for not being able to care for me, for not being there when I needed you…," etc.

6. **Repeat.** Have your client repeat the process for each painful thought, feeling, or memory.

REFLECT: A COUNSELING STORY

A twenty-year-old man named Tom came into my office and confessed that he had recently cheated on his wife. We talked about his life story, and when he told me about his relationship with his dad, I felt that his current situation had a lot to do with the trauma he experienced as a young boy in relation to his father. I asked the Holy Spirit, "Will you show Tom where the trauma came from?" After a few moments, he told me that his earliest childhood memory was of his brothers tied to a tree, getting beaten by their father with a belt. In the memory, Tom felt, "Dad loves them, but he's beating them…" and it became apparent to me that as a child, Tom had learned a perverted definition of love: Love is punishing. He subconsciously believed that intimacy is scary!

As he shared more of his story, here's what I learned: Despite his aversion to intimacy, he got married right out of high school, and because he'd never gotten healing, he sabotaged his marriage because of his belief that love eventually leads to pain. He believed that it was only a matter of time before he was rejected by his wife, so he subconsciously decided to reject her first by having an affair.

In the appointment, Tom didn't feel or show any emotion as he shared his memory with me, nor did he display any sort of emotion about the fact that he had cheated on his wife. Because of the incredible amount of pain that Tom experienced in his childhood, he had protected himself from "feeling" for years, which kept him from feeling fully known or loved by anyone, even his wife.

I knew that his emotions had to be unlocked in order for him to fully process the pain he'd experienced and come to a place of true forgiveness and freedom. So, I invited him to engage with the emotions of his earliest memory. I said to him, "I want you to close your eyes and connect with emotion. I want you to say to your dad what you feel in your heart as you watch him beat your brothers." At first, he had a hard time connecting with his emotions. He said, "Dad, I am not happy about this. It's mean." Because I could tell he was still disconnected from his emotions, I started speaking to Tom in way that would evoke a reaction. I said some really hard things like, "Tom, your dad didn't love you. He was mean and horrible to your brothers. Your brothers were in such pain as they were beaten. Tom, he made you sit there and watch as he hurt your siblings. How do you feel about that? What do you want to say to your father?"

After a few provocations, Tom finally exploded, and with his eyes closed, he began to yell at his father, "I hate you! Why were you not there for me? How could you have done this to my brothers? You are cruel and punishing!" After several minutes of Tom grieving in my office, he was done. He sat on my couch tired, crying for the first time in years, and more free of pain than he had ever been!

When Tom had calmed down, I asked him to repeat after me, "Holy Spirit, will you show me how You see my dad?" He responded that the Holy Spirit showed him his dad as a little baby. I asked him, "Tom, what does that mean to you?" He said, "My dad couldn't even take care of himself, much less my brothers and me." We continued to pray through this, inviting the Holy Spirit to minister to Tom's heart, until I could tell that he found true compassion for his dad. From that place of compassion, Tom was able to accept the fact that his dad really didn't know how to care for him, and he extended genuine forgiveness!

To continue Tom's process of healing, we renounced the lies he had believed about love being punishing, and we broke the spiritual partnership that he had made with fear. At the end of it all, although Tom had lost his marriage because of his brokenness, he felt empowered for the first time in his life to partner with Love and walk in freedom and wholeness.

What is the root issue causing Tom's inability to connect with his emotions?

_____

_____

_____

_____

_____

_____

_____

REFLECT: A COUNSELING STORY *(continued)*

What is the root issue that caused Tom to sabotage his marriage?

_____

_____

_____

_____

_____

With regards to this example, what is the connection between honest emotions and genuine forgiveness?

_____

_____

_____

_____

_____

What are some practical steps you would suggest that Tom take in order to fully walk out his repentance from the belief that "love is punishing?"

_____

_____

_____

_____

_____

People need to know that their emotions
are not a commentary on their character but
rather on how they feel in the moment.

REFLECT: A COUNSELING STORY

Once I ministered to a young lady named Ariel, that came up for prayer at the end of a church service who, unbeknownst to me, had been taken advantage of by a man when she was very young. She didn't disclose anything to me before I began praying, but when I started to pray for her, I could tell that she didn't love herself. Starting out, I quietly whispered to her, "Repeat after me... I love myself." She began to tremble as the pain inside of her welled up—pain that she had carried around for years, suppressed by the lies that held her bound.

With her chin quivering, she shamefully repeated the words after me, "I love myself." I then proceeded to say, "I'm fully loved!" Once again she took a deep breath, trying to control the emotions that were beginning to overwhelm her. "I'm fully loved," she said. Then I walked her through acknowledging her pain. She fought so hard to keep from feeling the anguish buried deep down inside, but I had her repeat after me, "I renounce the lie that it's not okay to feel pain. I renounce the lie that crying is weakness. I renounce the lie that it's not okay to think about what happened to me!"

At that point, I could tell that the pain of what had happened was beginning to overwhelm her. Her whole body shook, and she was about to say that she couldn't think about it, but I gently encouraged her to remember what had happened, assuring her that it was going to be okay.

I felt in my heart that she had experienced a horrible violation, so I said Ariel, "I want you to tell him in your mind how he made you feel!" She sat there, quietly with her eyes closed, and I could tell she was beginning to get angry and more emotional. I reassured her again that it was okay to say in her head everything she wished she could say to the man who hurt her about how she felt. Then, without warning, she burst out, yelling on the prayer line, "I hate you! I hate you for what you did to me! I hate you for stealing my innocence and for using peer pressure to trap me!" She went on like this for a while, and I let her go for it!

Once she was all done, she quieted down. At that point, I said to her, "I want you to ask the Holy Spirit how He sees this man." She paused for a bit, listening to the Holy Spirit, and then she said, "He loves him as much as He loves me!" She began to understand, even though she felt hatred and heartache about the man who violated her, that God loved him too, just like He loved her! It was an amazing revelation for her.

REFLECT: A COUNSELING STORY *(continued)*

After she allowed herself to connect with her pain, and after she acknowledged how she felt about what had happened to her, she was able to receive God's perspective, connect with compassion, and begin the process of forgiveness. I led her into the process of forgiveness by having her repeat after me, "I forgive you for violating me; I forgive you for stealing my innocence; I forgive you for taking what was not yours to take and for being selfish." I spent quite a while walking her through each violation that had happened, and at the end of it we prayed to bless him, and we prayed to bless her. For the first time in her life, Ariel broke the lies that held her bound—the lie that she was trash, the lie that she couldn't handle pain, and the lie that she needed to punish her perpetrator. She walked away that night feeling the freedom that true forgiveness offers us.

Thinking about Ariel's story, write down key moments that you recognize. What stands out to you, and what else would you coach her through, regarding repentance, processing pain, and forgiveness?

_____

_____

_____

_____

_____

Closing Keys

Genuine forgiveness leads to incredible amounts of freedom, and it is primarily attained when people connect with their pain, acknowledge their hurt, mourn their losses, and connect with compassion through the guidance of the Holy Spirit. This can take time, and it's our job as pastoral counselors to allow for the process to take place unto completion.

SECTION THREE

Create

Lesson Eight

A FIRM FOUNDATION

Creating Solutions

Identifying issues is the first stage in a pastoral counseling process. The second stage is the actual problem-solving stage during which you lead your clients through processes like repentance, working through pain, and forgiveness. These processes wipe the slate clean and tear down the old structures that kept them bound and trapped. The third and final stage in pastoral counseling involves creating new normals by replacing what was torn down in the previous stages with healthy ways of thinking. It's important not to leave your client alone to figure out what to do with their blank canvas. If left to ourselves, we will typically revert to old blueprints because they are the most familiar architecture.

This section will focus on how to help your clients create lasting solutions by reconstructing their framework and rewriting their "normal." It will walk you through how to teach people to use tools for health and proactively operate inside their new belief systems.

Laying a Firm Foundation

After tearing down old structures and clearing the landscape by thoroughly working through the processes of repentance, pain, and forgiveness, you can lead your clients into the reconstruction of a healthy, free, and sustainable life. Builders first lay a firm foundation, then build a solid structure.

The God Spot

One thing I've learned from my experience is that like when building a house, the most incredible power tool is useless to me if I'm not building on a firm foundation. There are God-sized needs in each of us that He intends to meet, but it's our job to recognize the needs that are there and invite God to be our source in these areas of our lives. He is meant to be our source for many things like identity, protection, provision, hope, comfort, healing, and unconditional love. For many, learning to trust God as our source in certain areas is quite a process! Knowing what it looks like to operate in this level of spiritual health can be difficult without a good picture to refer to. The best illustration I know of what it looks like to know God as the source can be found in Psalm 23. David *truly* knew God as his Protector, Provider, and Restorer! The result is that David was able to confidently walk through "the valley of the shadow of death" (the darkest, hardest of times) without fear![1] There's no *one* else and no-*thing* else other than God who will come through every time in these deepest areas of need.

Checking to make sure that your clients have a solid understanding of the role God is meant to play will help you ensure you're helping them build on a foundation that will last. If people don't know how to relate to God as their source in these deepest areas of need, they'll look to some*one* or some*thing* else to meet these needs. For example, if you don't confidently know God as the Provider, it's really scary when there's no money in your bank account! Likewise, if you rely on your significant other to convince you that you are "fearfully and wonderfully made," the thought of breaking up with him or her is terrifying, at best! Similarly, without resting in the assurance that you're worthy of love because God says so, insecurity creeps in every time you try to make a new friend for fear of rejection. The bottom line is this: If we don't have a solid foundation in God as our source for these very real needs in our lives, nothing that we build will stand.

As you're helping your clients pour their fresh, firm foundations, you can help them assess whether or not they've invited God to be their source in their areas of deep need. One indicator that God is not in the "God Spot" is that they have anxiety and fear. When they recognize an area where God is not their main source, take time to walk them through a simple process of repentance until God has been reinstated back to His rightful place. It may be helpful to revisit Lesson 5 as you guide your clients through repentance.

---

1 See Psalm 23 of the *English Standard Version*.

Building a Healthy Culture on the Inside

Once you know that you're building on a solid foundation with God in the right spot in people's hearts and minds, you can begin the process of building a new framework for health. As discussed in Lesson 3, there's a mindset and a belief system that gets people into unhealthy cycles in the first place! As such, if someone has battled with self-hatred for a long time, he can repent and invite God to be his source for identity and extend forgiveness to himself a million times. But if he doesn't get *rid* of the old mindset and change the way he thinks, he'll hold on to self-condemnation and will likely repeat the pattern of behavior. In Proverbs 23:7, the Bible says that whatever we believe in our hearts, we will act out.[2] So, after repenting and restoring belief to match God's design with Him as the source, the next step is to build a healthy culture on the inside. This process begins by creating new "normals" so that defaults change from unhealthy to healthy.

The diagram below provides a visual for what it can look like for a person to walk through a process of creating a new "normal" in foundational areas that need rebuilding. People can use the steps to adopt Biblical truth and watch it grow from a belief to a conviction, and into something that can be reproduced around them! We will address each step of this process and unpack what it looks like to thoroughly walk someone through this building phase.

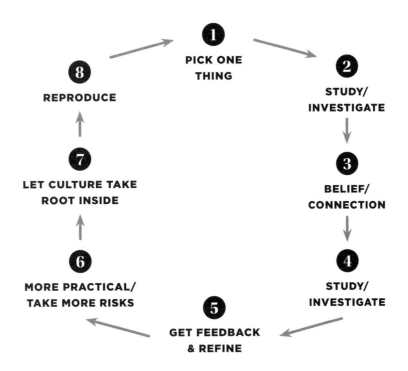

---

2 Proverbs 23:7 of the *New American Standard Bible* says, "For as he thinks within himself, so he is." See also Luke 6:45.

1. **Pick One Thing at a Time.** Building something new can be completely overwhelming if you are only looking at the big picture, but keep in mind that bricklayers lay one brick at a time. Whether people are merely repairing a section of their foundation or laying a new one altogether, taking one step at a time is the only way to ensure that the structure is built well.

   If someone has struggled with identity issues for a decade, there are likely *many* areas of their lives that have been impacted, causing them to act out in unhealthy ways. It's important to choose ONE unhealthy habit to fix at a time. For example, maybe they have recognized that when given a compliment, they always disregard it instead of embracing it and thanking the complimenter.

2. **Study & Investigate.** In order to change their bad habit in one specific area, your client will need to study and investigate the truth on this topic of identity! We discussed the concept of renunciation in Lesson 5, and it could be good to review this lesson to understand what it really means to replace lies with truth. Your clients can study the biblical truth, listen to podcasts, read books, or find personal heroes that operate in health in that subject area—anything that will help them gain understanding around the area they are trying to solidify. To keep with our example, in order to break the bad habit of disregarding compliments (a violation of knowing their identity in Christ), your client needs to study and investigate what the Lord has to say about our giftings, talents, and the fact that we're fearfully and wonderfully made in the image of Christ, Himself.

3. **From an Idea to a Conviction.** Truth has to move from our heads to our hearts and from an idea into a place of conviction. The Holy Spirit is the best Teacher, and if we commit ourselves to the Truth, it will move from an idea to an actual belief. To know the truth and BELIEVE it is different.

4. **Practice Makes Perfect.** This happens as we practice and take risks operating out of the truth. This can be trial and error! People need the opportunity to put into practice the knowledge they have gained because when our head knowledge and our experiences align, beliefs turn to deep conviction. Creating good habits in the place of old bad ones requires action, and repetition is key! Once a person has truth in his or her heart, it's important that they begin practicing acting out of this belief. Perhaps our hesitant-to-receive-compliments client begins simply by creating a script to use when given a compliment. They actually have to practice ACTING out of what they know is true in order to create a new normal. Take a look at this story to get a better understanding of the power of repetition and practice.

REFLECT: A COUNSELING STORY

I once met with a young man who believed that he was attracted to the same sex. For many years, he had battled with the shame of feeling attracted to other men, and the powerlessness of not knowing how to break out of that prison was eating him alive. As I listened to his story, I learned that when he was a kid, he was horribly bullied at school. Every day the other kids called him "gay" and heckled him to no end. To make matters worse, his parents were lost in their own world, disconnected from their son and his pain in this vulnerable season of life. Alone and hurting, this young man decided one day while walking to school, that if all of the other kids thought he was gay, he must be. After all, his parents weren't saying anything different! What we see, hear, and think every day eventually becomes what we embrace.

I spent several hours with this young man, teaching him how to work through pain and forgiveness, ultimately connecting him to Father God. By the end of our appointment, he was freed from the tormenting thoughts and blessed with truth and connection to God. However, because this young man had been oppressed for so long, I knew it was imperative that what happened in our counseling appointment would become a lifestyle and not a one-time experience. We talked at length about how to protect his mind from lofty thoughts and fill himself with truth and affirmation on a daily basis because it's positive repetition that will move conscious thoughts to subconscious ones that create habitual actions.

The kids told him that he was gay repeatedly until he believed them. This is exactly how his negative belief system was built. Our job is to reverse the process towards health, the same way it was created: through repetition.

5. **Get Feedback & Refine.** These kinds of processes aren't meant to be walked through alone! It's crucial that those seeking help invite others into their process so they can ask for feedback as they practice acting out of the truth in areas of former bad habits. When we invite people to watch our progress and give feedback, growth happens more quickly because we can make adjustments if needed, with the strength of others!

6. **More Practice Makes More Perfect.** After making adjustments and refinements, practice by taking more risks! Again, repetition is key!

7. **Let the Culture Take Root.** After a while, what was once done in obedience begins to flow naturally as the new, healthy culture actually becomes a part of who we are. After practicing receiving compliments over and over again, it will start to feel natural, and before you know it, your client that once rejected the notion they were worthy of any accolades will ACT in alignment with what they BELIEVE to be true in their heart.

8. **Reproduce.** It's at this point in the process that people begin to reproduce in their surrounding environment what is true in their own lives! We can give away and impart what we ourselves possess. Kingdom transformation happens when people who walk in health can give away their keys to other people.

Not only is this process useful for people who are working on empowering God to be their source, it will also help people become great at anything they put their minds to! If someone desires to become a better basketball player, they can follow these simple steps to grow in their skill! This tool will be one that you can hand out anytime you see your client needing to grow in a specific area.

REFLECT: A COUNSELING STORY

If you realize you have a hard time communicating without getting overly emotional and angry in the midst of conflict, how could you use the steps described above to become a healthier, more effective communicator? Use the steps outlined below to think through the process you'd walk through to grow in communication skills. What could you do at each step to gain ground?

1. Pinpoint **one growth area.**

   <u>**Communicating well in the midst of conflict.**</u>

2. **Study/investigate** until ideas become **beliefs/convictions.**

   _____

   _____

   _____

3. **Practice and take risks** to experience beliefs that move to convictions.

    _____

    _____

    _____

4. **Get feedback** from the community around you on how you're doing with implementation and **refine.**

    _____

    _____

    _____

5. **Practice and take more risks.**

    _____

    _____

    _____

――――

Willpower Versus Desire

As you help clients build, they will run into the temptation to partner with old mindsets and habits. You'll need to teach them how to choose well in those moments. It's important that you understand a little bit about willpower so you can empower them to use it when things get hard. Willpower is the ability to act according to our convictions, regardless of how we feel. Willpower is not something that we are born with or without! It's something that we grow, much like a muscle. Often times it's easy to get down on ourselves when we are not as strong in a particular area as we would like to be, but with a little practice and intentionality, we can actually strengthen our will.

There are a few keys that will help you understand how to empower someone to grow and use their willpower. Firstly, you must understand the difference between desire and happiness. People tend to think that the fulfillment of desires will ultimately lead to happiness. Not only is this untrue, it's actually a trap! When people work on making great life changes, it's common to feel desire for old ways of living or thinking.

For example, a man working to break free of addiction to pornography often desires to look at porn while abstaining. In order for this man to fully break the cycle of addiction, he will have to understand that his *desire* for porn will not lead him to *happiness* or complete fulfillment. Furthermore, he will have to accept the anxiety that comes from not giving in to his desires and remind himself that true fulfillment is going to cost him for a time. He will have to be pro-active and find something constructive to do with his time instead of medicating the anxious craving inside.

Let's look at eating habits as another example! Many people "wish" they would eat healthier, but because of the strong impulse toward comfort food, they tend to forfeit long-term happiness for a short-term reward. In order to counteract this behavior, it helps to connect with our wiser, future self that can ask you questions like, "Will I be happy next week for my decision today?" By connecting to your wiser, future self, you are able to will yourself in the right direction, accept the anxiety that comes from not meeting the immediate need, and look forward to the greater reward. The more connected we are to our future self, the more likely we are to reach our long-term goals.

To reward sacrifice is another great way to help people grow their willpower muscle. Simply put, when we give ourselves rewards for making good decisions, we want to make more good decisions! If you are trying to work out 3 days a week at the gym but you're struggling because you don't "feel" like doing it, find a reward that makes working out worth it. Momentum is created in our lives when we operate inside a system of healthy, positive reinforcement. When we aim ourselves at long-term happiness by living a life we're proud of rather than giving in to short-term fulfillment, we experience the benefit of exercising willpower, even when it's hard.

One last thing that is crucial to maintaining a strong will and becoming all that you were created to be is maintaining the ability to quickly forgive yourself and connect to self-compassion. Science shows that the quicker we are to accept our failures and forgive from a place of compassion, the quicker we will remember our long-term goals and get back on track.[3] When we use guilt and shame to try to move us back into order, we will experience the opposite result that we desire. Guilt and shame are bad motivators because they need to be medicated, leading you back into a destructive cycle of pain.

---

3 Taylor, R. (2017). *Willpower: Discover It, Use It and Get What You Want.* Hoboken: Wiley.

It's important that we don't try to survive on willpower alone, but add tools to our repertoire in order to maintain momentum when our willpower is low. When we rely solely on our will to move us forward, we are destined to fail. It's really simple. We were never meant to run only off of our willpower; when we do this, we exhaust our capacity and eventually revert back to our old behavior.

Your brain and your body should help you to remember your goals, override impulses, and manage stress. By practicing good habits, you can set yourself up for success and avoid unnecessary pitfalls.

No one can persuade another to change. Each of us guards a gate of change that can only be opened from the inside. We cannot open the gate of another, either by argument or emotional appeal."

MARILYN FERGUSON

Closing Keys

The process of reconstructing a person's life starts with ensuring a firm foundation is in place. In order for the foundation to withstand new framework, we must empower God as the source for our areas of deepest need. It's from a place of knowing God as your source for life that you can begin building new and healthy cultures on the inside of your clients. This is a process that is worth taking your time on! It's exciting to know that although the process includes laying one brick at a time, breakthrough in one area of a person's life often leads to a domino effect of breakthrough in other areas.

NOTES

_____

_____

_____

_____

_____

_____

_____

_____

_____

Lesson Nine
POWER TOOLS

Power Connection

Once you and your client have ensured that their foundation is strong and firm, you can move on to building the new structure! This is a very exciting stage in the pastoral counseling process because this is typically when your client finally has the capacity to visualize what a new life of freedom and health can look like. It's your role to empower and encourage your client to dream and visualize what you'll build together, and we know that although building something new can be exciting, it can also be a lot of work.

My friend and coworker Steve Backlund says, "Vision for the future gives power for the present."[1] This is so true! It's crucial that your clients can connect to the heart of God, dream about where they're headed, and visualize the beautiful, functional, finished product that's ahead of them. The Holy Spirit Himself desires to co-labor with us in our efforts toward living the life we were created for, so catching God's vision for our lives will keep us pressing forward when things get hard. As the counselor, strive to keep hope at the forefront of every part of the conversation. Real, lasting change will require your client to stay motivated to continually take a powerful position of ownership over every step of the building process! The highest quality power tools don't work at all unless connected to the power source.

---

1 Backlund, S. (2016, May 12). Empowering Beliefs About Others. Retrieved from http://ignitinghope.com/

Tools of the Trade

Just like you wouldn't send a construction worker onto a job site without knowing how to use their drills and saws, you don't want to send your clients into the building process without the knowledge of how to operate the necessary tools. The bulk of this lesson is like an owner's manual that someone would need to read to know how to wield the power-tools that will help in creating action plans that rebuild their lives.

Reconstruction can be a vulnerable process, and there is some safety equipment that will specifically help individuals know, value, and protect themselves while they work. There are also tools for building that will help them actually get the job done! In this lesson, we will go over how to use tools of the trade.

Self-Awareness

As previously mentioned in Lesson 4, self-awareness can be defined as the ability to know what is going on inside of you and how you are affecting those around you. Self-awareness comes more naturally to some people, and for others, it takes a lot of work to grow in self-awareness. If your client is not naturally self-aware, this is a tool you'll want to teach them how to use, as it is necessary for navigating reconstruction. In this lesson, it's my aim to unpack the tool of self-awareness on a deeper level.

Self-awareness is at the root of strong character and helps us find our authenticity, vulnerability, and trust. It reveals to us the pathways to our successes and failures, helping us map out safe roads for future travels. Self-awareness also helps us to stay in touch with what is happening inside of us throughout the day emotionally, physically, and spiritually. This is incredibly important when doing things like adopting new mindsets, proactively changing behaviors, expressing needs, and setting boundaries. Each person you counsel will need to be able to exercise self-awareness in order to build sustainably.

> *Self-awareness is not self-centeredness, and spirituality is not narcissism. 'Know thyself' is not a narcissistic pursuit.*
>
> **MARIANNE WILLIAMSON**

Here are 6 simple keys to growing in self-awareness:

1. **Pray.** The best place to start in a journey to self-awareness is asking the Holy Spirit to reveal subconscious thoughts and feelings to help us become more powerful.

   - What is going on inside of me that's making me feel this way?

   - What is the truth that I need to grab onto?

   - How do You see me?

   - How can I be more aware of my needs?

2. **Write down your main priorities and plans.** One of the most measurable ways to grow in self-awareness is to write down your highest goals. Writing things down in a journal or calendar makes it easy to check in on a daily basis. This will help you actually track your progress, and it will also help you become more aware of the vulnerabilities that keep you from meeting your goals.

3. **Know your triggers.** I find that many people fail to give attention to what triggers pain, hopelessness, and fear and are therefore ill-equipped when hard things happen. We discussed "Recognizing Red Flags" at length in Lesson 4. By knowing your points of pain, you can create a proactive plan ahead of time to identify red flags, enabling a powerful response rather than a powerless reaction.

4. **Take psychometric tests.** Personality, propensity, and aptitude assessments such as StrengthsFinder, Myers-Briggs, and DISC can be really helpful in giving you a map of how you tend to process information, make decisions, feel motivation, etc. The goal of these assessments is not that you would have results that validate dysfunctional behaviors. Rather, the results should empower you to understand yourself better, giving you language for why and how you do what you do, providing a basis for working on the areas of your life that need improvement and helping you embrace your areas of strength. Many of these assessments can be found for free online.

5. **Ask for input and feedback.** The Bible tells us, "Faithful are the wounds of a friend,"[2] and while no one wants to be wounded or hurt, it's important that the people we know and trust are able to give us healthy and helpful feedback. That your clients know how to

---

2 See Proverbs 27:6 of the *English Standard Version.*

ask for feedback from friends and trusted family is very important! While they may only see you once or twice, they will see their peer groups, friends, and family members on a regular basis! Accountability starts here. Here are a couple of questions you can give your clients to invite feedback:

- How do you experience me when we are with our friends?

- Can you tell me when I do that thing so I can learn to stop?

6. Check in with yourself throughout the day. Start each morning and end every evening by talking to yourself! Take a few minutes to find out how you are doing before you leave the house and at the end of the night. If talking to yourself is something that you forget to do, use your bathroom mirror as a place to write questions that will help you remember to check in with yourself! Ask simple questions like:

- How am I doing?

- What do I feel?

- Do I feel successful today?

- Did I care for myself today?

Celebrate successes of the day and acknowledge what you need to work on tomorrow.

Positive Self-Talk

In order for anyone to get whole, they must first learn to love themselves, no matter what. The Bible tells us to "Love your neighbor as yourself."[3] Many people miss the power of what this Scripture is actually saying. It is essentially saying, "If you cannot love yourself you will never be able to love other people." We must first possess the ability to extend unconditional love to ourselves through our thoughts, actions, and words before we can build in a healthy and sustainable way.

According to the National Science Foundation, we talk to ourselves at the rate of 150-300 words per minute, or nearly 50,000 thoughts per day. Of those words, 70% are negative, and 95% of all

---

3 See Mark 12:31 of the *New International Version.*

self-talk will be repeated the next day![4] Imagine how this mental self-talk will affect your actions, words, and the way you care for yourself! The results can be debilitating for even the most self-aware person. In order to move forward, your clients will need to practice and become skilled at positive self-talk.

There are a few passages of Scripture that speak to this concept:

"For as he thinks in his heart, so is he."

PROVERBS 23:7, NKJV

"A good man brings good things out of the good stored up in his heart,
and an evil man brings evil things out of the evil stored up in his heart.
For the mouth speaks what the heart is full of."

LUKE 6:45, NIV

"Do not be conformed to this world, but be transformed by the renewal of
your mind, that by testing you may discern what is the will of God, what is
good and acceptable and perfect."

ROMANS 12:2, ESV

The interesting thing about self-talk is that 70% of it is subconscious! That makes it even more important to implement Romans 12:2 and take every thought captive to the obedience of Christ. When you intentionally begin to pursue positive self-talk, you will find just how much negativity you have been allowing to swamp your thinking. God gives grace for what He asks us to do, so it is possible to renew your mind and be transformed, even in the way you internally think and speak about yourself.

There is only one variable between the people who have a strong sense of
love and belonging and those that don't. The people who have a strong
sense of love and belonging feel worthy of love!

BRENÉ BROWN

---

4 McIntosh, S. (2009). 50, 000 Angry Little Voices. In *The Battered Shield of Faith*. Xlibris, Corp.

Boundaries

The word "boundaries" has many connotations, and if you've ever been abused by someone's rejection or intrusion in the name of love, you might have an aversion to the word. However, boundaries are often given a bad rap if misunderstood. Having a good grasp on boundaries in our lives ensures that we know how to protect what's important to us, physically and emotionally. In order to build with sustainability, people *must* know how to assign the right boundaries after identifying their personal needs.

In Lesson 8, we discussed that everyone has a set of deep needs for which only God can be the source. There are, however, real and valid needs that each of us has that other people are meant to meet for us. Family and community are God's design! We all need to feel connected and unconditionally loved inside of relationship with other people, and if God is our SOURCE for unconditional love, we can actually receive unconditional love from other people as well. But relationships are only healthy and life-giving if boundaries are communicated and kept respectfully between parties. Relationally, boundaries don't keep people out; they are designed to *protect* your love for others!

Let's pretend for a minute that you live in a city where there have been some recent robberies. It's safe to say that most people would make sure that their doors were locked before leaving home for the day or going to bed at night in order to protect their home. When separated from the violations that have taken place, thanks to the front door and a deadbolt lock, it's relatively easy to connect to compassion if you consider that the burglars are just other hurting human beings who were someone's children at one point.

Everything changes, however, if a burglar actually enters your home and threatens your family's safety. As soon as someone uninvitedly crosses the boundary of your threshold and violates your sense of safety, it's a little harder to love them as someone else's hurting child. Am I right? This is a blown-up illustration of how boundary lines are actually meant to protect our love for others. Those who you trust should be allowed to get closer to your heart than perfect strangers.

The diagram on the next page provides a good visual for what it can look like to set up boundaries in your life to protect your relationships.

CIRCLES OF INTIMACY

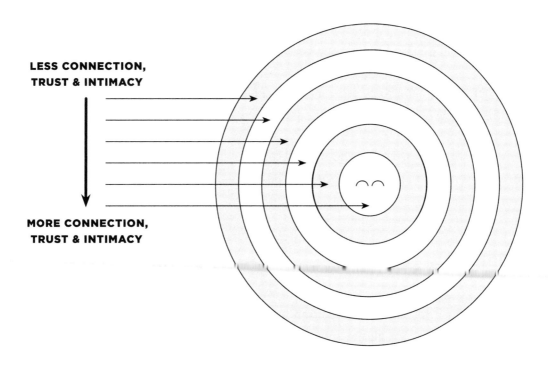

LESS CONNECTION, TRUST & INTIMACY

MORE CONNECTION, TRUST & INTIMACY

People in the outer rings are those with whom you have the least connection, trust, and intimacy. As you get closer to the center, the more connection, trust and intimacy in the relationship. Ultimately, God should be at the very center of your relational world. The lines between each relational realm are boundary lines. It's up to you to determine what you need in order for people to move closer to your heart.

Proverbs 25:28 of the New International Version says, "Like a city whose walls are broken down is a man who lacks self-control." Having a good handle on boundaries is essential in order to ensure that the walls of what you're building are strong. The person who lacks the ability to set good boundaries will end up like a broken-down, pillaged city. A defenseless city gets plundered and has nothing of value left to offer anyone. When your boundaries are removed, your treasure is gone! You can't set limits, you feel guilty, and you are easily manipulated by the threat of punishment. You are plundered by the people. A city without walls is not a place you will stay in for very long. Any army that wants to steal from you will run through, take what they want, and head out. With no boundaries or needs, there are no walls.

Here are some common mistakes people make in filling in this diagram:

- People put their spouse in the "God" spot.

- Many people put their kids in the same level of intimacy as their spouse.

- Certain personality types believe everyone is their "best friend," and their chart reflects that by having everyone they know listed in the 2nd or 3rd rung of the diagram.

If you would like more information about this, I recommend the book *Boundaries* by Henry Cloud and John Townsend, as well as the book *Keep Your Love On* by Danny Silk.

Concluding the Tools

Self-awareness, positive self-talk, and boundaries are how a person becomes aware of their inner worlds. This is what reveals the belief system they operate from, which is ultimately creating their reality.

REFLECT

Take a moment and fill out the different situations for yourself.

Relationships: Choose a relationship you have been in (romantic or platonic) where you constantly felt "not good enough," wrong, scared, overwhelmed, filled with anxiety, controlled, or shut down.

- **What does living in that type of relationship tell you about your worth and value?**

- **What are some of the reasons you would find yourself in a relationship like that?**

- **If you had a greater understanding of your boundaries, how to love yourself, what you believed and told yourself about you, would that relationship have happened?**

REFLECT(*continued*)

_____

_____

_____

_____

Work: Think of a job where you have felt continually pressured, pushed, overwhelmed, and undervalued.

- **What were the thoughts that would be going through your mind during the day?**

_____

_____

_____

_____

- **Why would someone think they could treat you in a manner that did not reflect value and respect for you?**

_____

_____

_____

_____

- **Do you set the tone for how you will be treated and what you are *worthy* of?**

_____

_____

_____

_____

- **Did you have boundaries that you protected and demanded others to respect, or were you a "wall-less city"?**

_____

_____

_____

_____

REFLECT*(continued)*

Life: What is the environment around you reflecting back to you about who you are? It is true that people treat us the way we expect to be treated. They gather this information from how we talk about ourselves, what we think we deserve, the importance and value we place on our lives and interests, and *the way we treat others.*

- **What are you noticing about your environments? What are they reflecting back to you?**

- **Is this consistent with what is true?**

The goal of this exercise is that you would be aware of your inner world to be able to help others identify what they think about themselves. Are they constantly comparing and breaking themselves down inside? Do they give unlimited, unreserved, and inappropriate access of themselves to those around them? How have their past relationships been? **These are all major "tellers of truth" in the self-love/boundaries world.**

Maintaining "Normal"

Whether you are aware of this or not, you know a feeling of "normal" throughout your day. This normal is sandwiched between anxiety and depression. This graph shows it below.

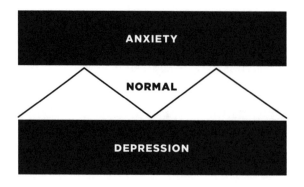

Knowing the place from which a person is operating is the jackhammer of all tools. This is the tool that reveals directly what emotions, feelings, and thoughts are being experienced.

In any given instance, a person is living in some relation to anxiety, depression, or, a place we would call normal. The littlest things can launch a person into anxiety and drop them into depression, such as the house being dirty, a wrong tone in someone's voice, or a smell. Living in a high level of anxiety increases stress, causes adrenal fatigue and makes those around you hate life. Anxiety puts you on high alert and is not conducive to a successful day of peace, joy, and health. Depression is its own world of hopelessness and wreaks all sorts of havoc on our bodies. Being self-aware enough to see if you are headed for an anxiety or depression cliff is a life saver.

So often the triggers are little. They seem silly, but they pile up so steadily that before someone knows it, they are full blown in an anxiety attack or depression slump. Maintaining a healthy "normal" is maintaining balance, peace, and truth. Boundaries, self-awareness, self-talk, and self-love are all crucial players in this process.

REFLECT

Scenario: It's Monday morning. You wake up from having a bad dream. This dream was you missing your alarm! You awake in a panic to find you have 45 more minutes to sleep. Your heart pounding in your chest, you are unable to go back to sleep. Your head is racing with thoughts about what would have happened if your dream had been true. You then get ready for work as you are experiencing tension in the house. Your spouse is not happy with you for some reason, your kids have attitude again, your kitchen is a mess, and to top it off, it's raining outside.

As you leave for work, your "normal" is slowly climbing up into anxiety. Each interaction you have makes it increase. By the time you are in your car, you are frustrated. You don't know why, but you're mad. Your kids want to listen to the radio, loudly. You forgot your lunch. The drop-off line is long. You are staring at the clock as it climbs nearer and nearer to you "being late for work, i.e. failing." You arrive at work, 3 minutes late. You run inside, anxiety peaked. Your head is spinning with words mixed between your anger of other people and how mad you are at yourself. Your boss walks in, throws your report back on your desk, and says it isn't right. It's not even bad, but "it's wrong" is what you hear! "You failed. You are a screw-up. Your family hates you. You can't!"

REFLECT *(continued)*

even do the one thing you should be able to, sleep peacefully!" are the thoughts running through your subconscious.

At this moment, your anxiety spikes to a high peak and drops rapidly into depression. You are no longer flustered and mad. You are depressed. You don't want to try anymore. You feel defeated. There is no light at the end of this tunnel. You think of your marriage, how hopeless it feels. You think of your family, how out of control they are. The thoughts then spiral downwards, and your self-talk gets worse.

At the end of the day, you make it home. Your spouse is wanting your attention and for you to "be present," but all you feel is detached. You're not even aware of what happened. You always feel like this. Everyday.

This is a classic example of what happens on a daily basis. Anxiety and depression are sneaky and pull us into them if we are not aware!

Anxiety and depression are interchangeable with triggers. At any given moment, we can be "triggered" and launched into a world we were not even aware we were heading toward. Being aware of this is such an important tool.

Ask your client what "triggers" them. Walk through an average day with them, hear the events and look for the clues that anxiety and depression are increasing.

They may think they have a massive issue with depression but really it's that they are not self-aware. They need to keep track of their thought life and what is happening inside. Acknowledging anxiety and/or the feelings of depression is so powerful. When you are aware of something, it no longer has the upper hand. Even if the scenario from above was not changed, if the person was aware of their anxiety and depression increasing, they could keep themselves grounded. They could choose peace. They could look at the circumstances and decide to be calm.

Closing Keys

In this lesson, I handed you some important tools for your toolbelt and for those you are leading into health and freedom. These tools are specifically designed to aid in the reconstruction process so that what your clients build is strong enough to last. Knowing how to stay connected to vision and the voice of the Holy Spirit, operate in mature self-awareness, care for yourself with positive self-talk, and set healthy boundaries are the power-tools needed to build with integrity.

NOTES

_____

_____

_____

_____

_____

_____

_____

_____

_____

_____

_____

_____

_____

_____

_____

_____

_____

_____

_____

_____

_____

_____

Lesson Ten

RECONSTRUCTION

Committing to the Process of Reconstruction

As you become good at utilizing all of the skills we have discussed in this manual and leading people through the different stages of counseling and healing, you will need to develop a plan with them for their future. When Moses led the Israelites out of the wilderness, it was not very long before they became weary of the journey and wanted to go backward.[1] Why do you think that is? I think people are often afraid of what they don't know and cannot see. It's normal and common for people to choose familiar pain and dysfunction because they have learned to live there in a measure of predictability and safety. We know, however, that doing the same thing over and over again, expecting or hoping for a different result, is insanity!

People need to be able to follow an action plan that will take them in a new direction, or else they'll wander back to familiar paths. It's your job as the counselor to help create a recipe for success after giving them access to all the right ingredients. It's the client's job to choose to follow the recipe and see it through to completion.

Think about it like this: On the third day of taking antibiotics after a nasty bout of strep throat, the pain associated with the sickness is mostly gone, but doctors tell you to finish the antibiotics to ensure the infection is killed. As the patient, it might be tempting not to take the rest of the pills, but this will present a problem if the sickness returns because when it does, the antibiotics may no longer

---

1 See Numbers 14.

work and the infection could very well be stronger than before!

A person in counseling can experience something similar. People often experience a taste of freedom, feel alive for the first time in a long time, and decide to abandon the prescription for health. As a counselor, ensure that your client is committed to the entire process in order to see lasting results that can be reproduced in the environment around them. After all, our goal is exponential growth, generation to generation!

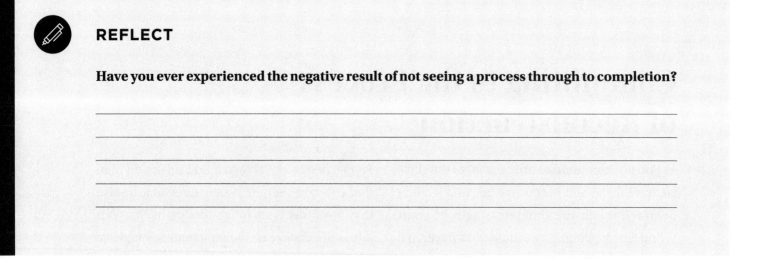

REFLECT

Have you ever experienced the negative result of not seeing a process through to completion?

_____

_____

_____

_____

_____

There is nothing like returning to a place that remains unchanged
to find the ways in which you yourself have altered.

NELSON MANDELA

Creating Action Plans

Creating a good plan of action for a client is actually quite a heroic act! It helps turn dreams into reality and mountains of obstacles into clear pathways. An action plan sets people up for long-term success by giving them day-by-day steps. John J. Beckley, a 18th-century American political leader, said, "Most people don't plan to fail, they fail to plan."[2] Nobody wants to fail, but without a clear action plan including clear steps to take toward success, your clients will have a difficult time achieving lasting breakthrough. You want every client you help to leave your appointments with a tailor-made action plan that's easy to understand and possible to achieve. This lesson is designed to help you learn how to create action plans.

You are like a trainer in the gym, there to give someone the right combination of exercises to help them achieve their desired results. Your job is to be straightforward, confident, and full of hope for their situation. In Lesson 9, we discussed the importance of hope and vision for someone getting whole, and that emphasis will be even more important in building the action plan. A client will refer to their action plan long after they end their sessions with you. It should be a beacon of hope in their most difficult places.

Considerations Before Creating an Action Plan

1. **Refer back to your notes.** In order to create a plan that will work for your client, you must consolidate some key information you've gathered during your previous sessions with your client. Take note of the following:

   - What is the main problem? (Refer back to Lesson 2.)

   - What is their belief system, and where did it originate, and how does it play out in their life? What are their cycles? (Refer back to Lesson 3.)

   - Have your client explain to you again what their root issue is. If your client is unable to explain his own root issue, it will be impossible for him to successfully navigate through his action plan. The better we understand ourselves, the greater success we will have in meeting our needs and walking out our healing. (Refer back to Lesson 4.)

---

2 Halpern, B. (2015). *Supercharge Your Emotions to Win: 7 Keys to Achieve the Life You Desire and Deserve.* S.l.: BPS Books.

- What are your client's biggest trigger points, and how would you label them as red flags? (Refer back to Lesson 4.)

2. **Never underestimate the power of hope.** You must ensure that your client knows how to connect to hope. Hope, in my opinion, is probably one of the most underestimated, overlooked factors in the well-being of an individual. My own journey has proven the power of belief beyond all odds, and also the dark side of being hope deprived. Take a look at this study and what scientific research has said about hope in a summary written by Isaiah Hankel in his book, *Black Hole Focus*:

> *In the 1950s, Curt Richter, a Harvard graduate, and Johns Hopkins scientist did a series of experiments that tested how long rats could swim in high-sided buckets of circulating water before drowning. Dr. Richter found that, under normal conditions, a rat could swim for an average of 15 minutes before giving up and sinking. However, if he rescued the rats just before drowning, dried them off and let them rest briefly, and then put them back into the same buckets of circulating water, the rats could swim an average of 60 hours! If a rat was temporarily saved, it would survive 240 times longer than if it was not temporarily saved. This makes no sense. How could these rats swim so much longer during the second session, especially just after swimming as long as possible to stay alive during the first session? Dr. Richter concluded that the rats were able to swim longer because they were given hope. A better conclusion is that the rats were able to swim longer because they were given energy through hope. The rats had a clear picture of what being saved looked like, so they kept swimming.*[3]

If you think about it, hope was a catalyst for vision, willpower, and perseverance, the importance of which we discussed at the beginning of Lesson 9. We are not much different than those rats swimming in a pool of water. The question is, are you swimming in a pool of hope or hopelessness?

After a decade of counseling, I've come to realize that you can give the best advice, tools, and even encouragement to a client, but unless they possess enough hope to carry themselves through the hard times, your best effort will not be good enough. The challenge here is probably obvious. How do we instill hope into people? My father always says, "What we cultivate will dominate!" It's up to each individual to steward their thoughts in such a way that they cultivate a culture of hope. It's more than wishful thinking or having

---

3 Hankel, I. (2015). *Black Hole Focus: How Intelligent People Can Create a Powerful Purpose for Their Lives.* Chichester, West Sussex, United Kingdom: Capstone.

good thoughts. The goal is that each client would build a case for hope in their life. This often means that they will need to acknowledge that their past experiences are not the highest truth, but that they are open to a greater reality—God's reality!

Keep in mind that without a strong undercurrent of hope, no action plan will yield the desired results. And conversely, the more hope infused into the plan, the better the results!

3. **Consider using S.M.A.R.T. Goals.** Within an action plan, you want to identify success and create goals that your client can meet to measure success and growth. One of the simplest and most-used charts for creating personal growth is the S.M.A.R.T. Goals system, which can help you create a viable, comprehensive plan. You can download many different templates for S.M.A.R.T. Goals on the internet, but here are the main components:

S.M.A.R.T.	QUESTIONS TO ASK
SPECIFIC *Simple, Sensible, Significant*	*-What do I want to accomplish?* *-Why is this goal important?* *-Who is involved?* *-Where is it located?* *-Which resources or limits are involved?*
MEASURABLE *Meaningful, Motivating*	*-How many?* *-How much?* *-How will I know I've accomplished it?*
ACHIEVABLE *Agreed, Attainable*	*-How can the goal be accomplished?* *-What are the logical steps I should take?*
RELEVANT *Reasonable, Realistic, Results-Based*	*-Is this a worthwhile goal?* *-Is this the right time?* *-Do I have the necessary resources to accomplish this goal?* *-Is this goal in line with my long-term objectives?*
TIME-BOUND *Time-Limited, Time-Sensitive*	*-When will I work on this goal?* *-How long will it take to accomplish this goal?* *-When is the completion of this goal due?*

The completion of a S.M.A.R.T. Goals chart cannot be the entire action plan, but it is a good foundation for the action plan to be built upon.

4. **Make sure that your client has accountability and community.** Real accountability is only present in our lives when we have a personal relationship with people who can and do speak into our hearts, our circumstances, and our relationships. Everyone needs these deep, covenant connections, not primarily because they keep us from failing, but because they inspire us to reach for the high call of God that rests on each of our lives. Historically, "accountability plans" were thought of as a system of checks and balances set in place to help people refrain from destructive behavior. However, restraining poor behavior should be the byproduct of living out your God-given potential.

We all need to be accountable to people who regularly remind us that we were born to make history. We are called to give an account for our ability, not our disability! When we live connected to community, we are able to glean from the strength and wisdom of the people around us to reach our short and long-term goals. In order for action plans to work, each client needs to know who's in their court. Help your client identify who, besides you, is their accountability and community who will help them along in their journey.

A Tailor-Made Plan

The best action plans are ones that the client helps to create. I've heard it said, "we protect what we help build!" When creating a plan, I like to put the problem and root issue in front of the client and ask them to brainstorm some solutions. Sometimes it's helpful to have them spend some time away from you thinking through this. From here, I expand on what they have already come up with.

Aside from these basic keys mentioned above, the best way for me to teach you how to create custom-made action plans for your clients is by sharing examples with you. The following counseling story will provide a great framework for how to create action plans for your clients.

REFLECT: A COUNSELING STORY *A Struggle with Pornography*

Joe came into my office because of a struggle with pornography. We found that his real issue was a fear of intimacy. His negative belief system said that sharing your feelings is "girly" and weak. Although Joe grew up in a decent home, he recognized that his parents were emotionally shut down and unable to validate his masculinity or provide a healthy sense of intimacy for him. Because of this, Joe had been oblivious to his own personal needs and the needs of others. This resulted in Joe being incredibly lonely and ashamed of himself as a man because of his inability to control himself. After several meetings, Joe realized that he had always been afraid of intimacy, especially with other men, and he understood that pornography was hindering his social, mental, and spiritual life. He was aware of the problem at hand, had repented from his old ways of thinking, and felt ready to walk toward health and freedom.

My first step in creating an action plan for someone struggling with pornography would be to take all of the above information and assess the greatest area of need. As we discussed in Lesson 8, people do best when they work on one thing at a time and in Joe's case, his fear of intimacy was his greatest area of need. From there, my plan for Joe would be really simple.

I would start by having Joe recognize the needs he does have and validate them every day. There are several ways to do this. My favorite way is to have a client write on their mirror a few questions that they read every day. If Joe reads and answers these questions in the morning and evening, he should be able to assess his progress and make any necessary changes in order to be able to care for himself well. Joe would also want to write the truth about who he is as a man, and about intimacy on his mirror. Every morning, Joe needs to begin to fill his mind with the truth about who he is and what he needs.

From here, Joe should begin to act upon what he is finding out that he needs. One of the best places for Joe to practice getting needs met would be a men's purity group or a similar setting. By attending such a group, Joe would be able to interact with men who love him regardless of his imperfections, as he learns to love himself. Furthermore, he would have a safe place to share his needs, feelings, and shortcomings. When Joe messes up, he is able to quickly confess, repent and get right back on track inside of community. Also, when Joe notices his "red flags," he will have someone to reach out to for help before it becomes a forest fire. As Joe progresses in his healing, our goals and plans will change. It's likely that I would have him read books, listen to teachings and podcasts, and talk to other men who have overcome what he is facing.

Take a look at the diagram below, which might help you visualize what it can look like to create a plan of action with your client that they can take with them when they leave your office.

ACTION PLAN	NOTES
PROBLEM	*Porn Addiction*
BELIEF SYSTEM	*"Intimacy is scary."* *Came from not having his needs validated as a kid*
GREATEST NEED	*Intimacy*
TRIGGER POINTS/RED FLAGS	*Loneliness, isolation, shame*

TO DO:

Work on validating your needs.
Write on your mirror a few key phrases to help you discover how you're doing on the inside and what you need that day. Answer these questions morning and night for 2 weeks until we meet next. Use phrases like:

- *How am I doing today?*
- *What do I feel?*
- *Who should I tell?*

Practice getting your needs met in a healthy way.
Sign up for and attend the Men's Purity Group every Monday night. This is a 6-month commitment where you can practice sharing your feelings and deepest needs inside of friendship. This will also help you learn how to lend strength to others.

Make a plan for your red flags.

- **Loneliness/Isolation** - Pick one person that you trust who you are going to reach out to when you discover feelings of loneliness. Let this person know ahead of time so that when you contact them, they know the context. Decide ahead of time what you will do together to create healthy connection when you're feeling lonely or are tempted to isolate.

- **Shame** - Choose one or two scriptures that speak the truth about your worth and identity in Christ. Write them on notecards that you will strategically place: in your car or on your desk, or set a reminder on your smartphone, etc. When feelings of shame creep in, stop them in their tracks with the Truth.

Do homework for overcoming shame.
Download and listen to "The Power of Vulnerability" by Brené Brown.

It's important to note that clients can easily become overwhelmed by plans that are too elaborate. Remember, there's no use in biting off more than they can chew! Take one step of the journey at a time. For example, if a client is struggling with self-hatred, and they think that it would be helpful to write down what they like about themselves every day, let them start there! Assess the capacity of the person you're working with and the depth of their issue. It's common for counseling processes to take months or even a year.

As time goes on, I would slowly add to or change the workload as I am able to assess what is working and what's not. This is where it is helpful to have multiple resources and more than one plan. You will find that what worked great for one person didn't do much for another. This is because each individual is incredibly unique in personality and upbringing. By constantly checking in, you should have a good idea if the prescription is working or if it needs to change.

REFLECT

Scenario: Sophia has struggled off and on with overeating since she was a young girl. She grew up in foster care, constantly moving from place to place. Sophia knows that powerlessness is her "normal" because of the instability she experienced in her childhood. She has recognized that she often feels out of control when she experiences big changes, when she travels, and when she is by herself for long periods of time. These situations often trigger her into her cycle.

With the information above and what you have learned about the counseling process, fill in the To-Do section of the worksheet on the next page as if you were handing Sophia her action plan for the first stage of her healing process. As always, there are many ways to handle every type of issue. Feel free to explore and even research how to help people struggling with this type of issue. In doing so, you'll teach yourself how to think outside of the box as well as identify what questions you still need answers to in order to help someone like Sophia.

ACTION PLAN	NOTES
PROBLEM	Eating disorder
BELIEF SYSTEM	"Life is out of my control." Started as a young girl in an unstable environment.
GREATEST NEED	To overcome powerlessness
TRIGGER POINTS/RED FLAGS	Change, traveling, loneliness... fear

TO DO:

Recharge!

Over the years, I've noticed a common theme that I think deserves mentioning. Almost without fail, when someone is in crisis, sin, overwhelmed, or just working hard to improve their personhood, the most common response is to completely remove "fun" from life and focus all efforts on the problem at hand. For the sinner, if he walks around downcast in shame, the environment around him is convinced that he really is "sorry" because they can see sorrow on him. Yet if that same man/woman repents, creates a plan for freedom, and exudes joy, that same environment becomes skeptical of the repentance because common belief is that people who sin should look sad for an extended period of time, especially if the sin is great. Likewise, a person who is in crisis simply doesn't have the time to include fun into their life—after all, they're in crisis!

From afar, this looks really responsible and even noble; however, there is nothing further from the truth! The God we serve gives us beauty for ashes, joy for mourning, a spirit of praise for heaviness. His joy is our strength, and when we are weak, He makes us strong. In James 1:2 of the New International Version, we are exhorted to see our trials as "pure joy," knowing that the perseverance that comes from trials lead us to completion in Christ.

An action plan that doesn't include joy, fun, excitement and even adventure is bound to fail! **Joy is to the soul what rest is to our physical body**; it's the way we recharge. Years ago, motivated by the movie *"300,"* I decided that I was going to start working out. With the goal of being "ripped," I took my little 155lb frame to the gym and started in heavy. After just a few days, I could tell I was on track due to my inability to move a muscle. My entire body was experiencing the consequences of my enthusiasm without sound knowledge. My belief going into the weightlifting world was this: Go as many times as possible and lift as much weight as you can. It just seemed logical!

After a few months of going to the gym consistently, I met a man named Danny. Danny was that "guy" that we all want to look like. He basically set the bar for every other man in the gym. After watching Danny work out for a month or so, it was obvious to me that he and I had the same goal, but a much different approach. In a conversation one day, Danny began to explain to me that rest was just as important as work. In fact, he said that without resting, I was just being counterproductive. In order for muscle to grow, it needs time to heal in between workouts. Without adequate time to heal, I was just breaking down precious muscle. After 6 months of sticking to a healthy workout plan, I had gained 20+ pounds of muscle and was in the best shape of my life!

There is little difference between what I did physically in the gym and what we need to do emotionally in order to live a healthy, sustainable life. Joy, hope, adventure, and fun all make the hard times bearable. The more challenging the season is, the more hope and joy a person is going to need because of the tremendous output of energy. Furthermore, if someone is going to sustain a long-term process of working hard, they are going to need to recharge daily. Remember, going from glory to glory is a process, and life's a marathon, not a sprint. In order to run this race, let's make sure to set healthy expectations for yourself first, and then the ones we are working with!

Closing Keys

It is both an honor and a privilege to encourage and strengthen others in their journey toward emotional health. Setting them up for long-term success is a very important piece of the process. The goal is to leave them in a place where they feel both equipped and inspired to continue forward. This will come from making sure they understand their own journey, triggers, and goals. They need to be able to embrace their story with the lens that their past is a piece of what makes them beautiful. They also need to feel excited about the goals they have ahead and understand how to achieve them.

It is always important to remember that life is a journey, and not a destination point! Therefore, set your client up for success by talking through their outlets for enjoying life. Counseling is not a linear process, nor often measurable day by day. It is about stepping into someone's story and pain and giving them tools to see and move through to the other side with the hope that they can actually make it.

NOTES

NOTES